Coursework

To the Head of Business Studies

Accounting Programs

For the BBC Microcomputer

M. K. Southworth

A suite of three
Accounting Programs
1. Double-entry bookkeeping
2. Final accounts of a sole trader
3. Budget

Causeway Press Ltd

Causeway Press Ltd
PO Box 13, Ormskirk, Lancashire L39 5HP
© Diane Wallace, 1987
1st Impression 1987

British Library Cataloging in Publication Data

Wallace, Diane
    Coursework in business studies and commerce.
    1. Commerce   2. Business education
    I. Title
    380.1   HF1008
    ISBN 0-946183-37-6

Phototypesetting by Chapterhouse, The Cloisters, Formby, L37 3PX
Printed and bound by Scotprint Ltd., Musselburgh, Scotland

CONTENTS

Acknowledgements

The author would like to thank Stephanie Wallace for creating the character of Dick Clever.

Thanks are also due to Gerry Gorman for his contribution of thoughts and ideas to chapters 3 and 4; and to the pupils of Ridley High School, Blyth and Tynedale High School, Blyth for permission to use their work.

Cover, graphics and Dick Clever drawings by Allen Associates.
Cartoons by Antony Winterbottom.

We are grateful to the following for permission to reproduce copyright material.

Burberrys Ltd. p. 64
Controller of Her Majesty's Stationery Office p. 45
CUS Transport Ltd. p. 15
Daily Express p. 53
Exchange & Mart p. 55
Guardian Newspapers Ltd. p. 48, p. 54
House of MayFair Ltd. p. 62, p. 82
Lloyds Bank plc p. 63
Nissan Motor Co. Ltd. p. 15

Every effort has been made to locate the copyright owners of material quoted in the text. Any omissions brought to our attention are regretted and will be credited in subsequent printings.

Teacher's Introduction

This book is a practical guide for pupils doing coursework assignments. It is designed to provide guidance on every aspect, and at every stage, of the coursework component of GCSE Business Studies and Commerce courses.

The GCSE Committee for Business Studies has stressed the importance of pupils' ability to demonstrate the use of facts and data in a practical way and emphasises the importance of verbal response for some pupils. (*SEC News*, No 3, Summer 1986). Coursework is being used increasingly as a learning strategy and the guidance given in this book is applicable to long and short projects, written and non-written presentations.

The text is interspersed with a large number of short exercises which aim to encourage pupils to develop and practise the skills used in practical assignments. In addition to the section devoted to examples of coursework assignments, there is a wide range of ideas scattered throughout the book which can be developed into coursework projects.

The aim of this book is to guide the pupil in planning, investigating and presenting coursework assignments. It is hoped that the book can be used in a variety of ways: read through and discussed rather like a traditional textbook; issued to pupils to work through at their own pace; or used selectively by pupils whenever they need help with a particular aspect of their coursework.

1 What is coursework . . . and why bother doing it?

...IN ITS BROADEST SENSE...
COURSEWORK IS WORK
DONE DURING A COURSE!

What do you think coursework is?

Is it

- tasks you have done by yourself in class?
- work you have completed as a member of a group?
- short assignments set by the teacher?
- long assignments which have to go to the examinations board?
- investigations you have carried out away from the classroom?
- a project you may have been set?
- something as ordinary as homework?

It is all of these – Dick was right! – it **is** work done during a course and different types of work can have different purposes, uses and advantages.

But why should you bother doing coursework? Let's have a look at some of the advantages which coursework can offer.

...COURSEWORK CAN MAKE THE SUBJECT REAL...

We tend to believe that everything we read in textbooks describes the real world, but this is not always the case.

Exercise 1

Which type of business organisation would be best for the following firms?
a) the manufacturer of golf accessories;
b) distributors of frozen chickens;
c) ladies' and men's hairdresser.

You can probably answer these questions by looking for the main characteristics of the different types of business organisations in any Business Studies or Commerce textbook and deciding which one best fits the examples in the question. But how can you be sure that the answers in the textbooks are always right? Each one of the firms given in the exercise is exceptional in that it does not follow the general rule.

a) The manufacturer of golf accessories is a **sole trader**! The firm consists of one lady who makes furry headcovers for golf clubs. She is self-employed and occasionally employs one or two 'out workers' on a casual basis as the need arises.

b) The firm which distributes frozen chickens is a **partnership**. There are two young men who 'work the markets' and operate on a very small scale indeed.

c) The hairdressing firm is a **limited company** owning five very successful shops.

Did you answer the question correctly? Probably not – but it was not a very fair question as the examples were not typical – but they were real! Coursework can show that the real world is not as simple or as neat and tidy as the textbooks sometimes suggest.

Exercise 2

As a piece of coursework you could identify some of the businesses in your area, suggest what types of organisation they may be, and then check up for yourself. This kind of coursework **makes the subject real** – and quite often the reasons for being a sole trader/partnership/limited company etc are quite fascinating . . . !

Some people are really good at writing essays and can explain exactly what they mean – other people can't and it's not fair to expect everybody to be able to show how much they know or understand by producing written work. Suppose you were set an assignment to describe the distribution of wholemeal flour. You don't need to write an essay – you could make a storyboard or if you can't draw very well you could cut out pictures from magazines or even take photographs. You can **show** everybody concerned how much you know about the distribution of wholemeal flour **and** how much work you have done.

... COURSEWORK MAKES TOPICS MORE INTERESTING ...

OK, so the syllabus states that you must know the boring facts about different methods of production. How can coursework make this more interesting? Easy, look at the production methods of firms which appeal to you. For example, you could decide to investigate production methods in a chemical firm because there is one near to where you live, or because your uncle works there or because you like doing chemistry. Or, if you've got a sweet tooth, you might enjoy the investigation shown in the cartoon.

... COURSEWORK GIVES YOU THE FREEDOM TO FIND OUT WHAT YOU WANT TO KNOW ...

Some parts of the course may interest you more than others and you may want to find out more about a particular topic. Coursework gives you freedom to reach the depths that classwork doesn't! Suppose you want to be an electrician when you leave school, and at present you are learning about labour as a factor of production. You could do yourself a favour and extend your studies by doing an investigation into the employment opportunities and training facilities for electricians in the firms in your local area.

In all your subjects you will have to use certain skills such as written communication, discussing, researching etc. You can use coursework to practise these skills before they are assessed. For example, in GCSE English you may be assessed on your ability to give a short talk. You can practise this by reporting back to your class or group the results of an investigation in Business Studies or Commerce.

Sometimes collecting information can be really tedious – especially when you have to plough your way through boring books with small print and no pictures. If you tackle the fact-finding task as a group you'll finish more quickly – and you might even have some fun!

When you're learning about a certain topic it's sometimes easy to forget the relevance of that topic. When you're studying different parts of the syllabus the whole course is broken down into a series of separate topics. Coursework fits the topics together. For example, you might have been studying transport; sources of finance; recruitment of labour; pressure groups – all as separate topics. A piece of coursework investigating the location of a firm specialising in paint and cellulose spraying could bring all of these topics together.

So you see, depending upon what the coursework is being used for it will take a different form. Just like a Private Eye – sometimes he'll be able to solve his case using books and newspapers, sometimes he can stay in his nice, warm office and use the telephone or telex, but sometimes he may have to get out and do some legwork – it just depends on the individual problem.

Now you have an idea about what coursework is you should try it for yourselves. Don't take my word for it – good detectives always check it out for themselves!

2 Starting research

WANTED

ENTHUSIASTIC DETECTIVES
who are very curious about lots of things
and like finding out
FOR THEMSELVES

The successful applicants will be friendly, polite and
have a good sense of humour. An ability to
distinguish facts from opinions would be a distinct
advantage — and so would a basic knowledge of
Business Studies or Commerce.

DEFECTIVE DETECTIVES NEED NOT APPLY!

If your application is successful you will benefit
by becoming experts in coursework and so
improve your grades in subjects other than
Business Studies or Commerce.

The advertisement above outlines some of the qualities and attitudes which will help you get the most out of your coursework. Research is like detective work – the outcome of the investigation will depend upon the quality of the evidence collected. If you don't have the right attitude and tackle your coursework in a half-hearted way then you'll probably miss lots of clues and evidence. But if you have the right approach then the evidence you collect, or **data** as we shall be calling it, will be **high quality**.

ENTHUSIASTIC · INDEPENDENT · CURIOUS · FRIENDLY · POLITE · SENSIBLE

Exercise 1

The advertisement mentions just some of the qualities which may help you when you are doing coursework. In what ways do you think these qualities can help? Can you think of any other qualities which may be an advantage?

Could YOU apply to be a detective? Do YOU have some of the personal qualities mentioned above? Do YOU have the right attitude? – or would you be a defective detective?

You'd be surprised at the minimum requirement for doing coursework. Answer the following questions – truthfully – and see if you could become a successful applicant . . .

MAKE A NOTE OF THE BOX WHICH APPLIES TO YOU

	YES	NO
Can you read?	☐	☐
Can you write?	☐	☐
Can you ask questions?	☐	☐
Do you have any experience at all of life outside school?	☐	☐
Do you know where to find books and newspapers?	☐	☐
Can you recognise when you need help?	☐	☐
Are you interested in anything?	☐	☐
Have you ever made a decision?	☐	☐
Are you following a course in Business Studies or Commerce?	☐	☐
Would you like to enjoy your work more?	☐	☐

If you answered YES to all of the questions then you will be an excellent investigator.

If you answered YES to 5 or more of the questions then you'll probably need some help to become an excellent investigator.

If you answered NO to 5 or more of the questions then you're probably a lost cause but you could still enjoy the social side of coursework!

No matter how well you scored in the quiz, you will probably need help to organise your investigation – even detectives have to learn!

Has the teacher really given the student 'a start'?

Not really – advertising is much too big an area for the student to be able to 'go away and get on with their coursework' – isn't it?

To make life easy – and we're all in favour of this – there needs to be a starting point which can be used in all investigations. Once an investigation has been started it becomes quite easy – like lots of tasks starting is the hard part. Detectives always have the same starting point . . . they ask the question 'Who dunnit?' They then answer the question as best they can at the time depending upon how much information they have, for example,

   – 'who?' . . . the butler;
   – 'dunnit?' . . . pinched the silver.

You need to ask a question like this and the answer to the question will be your starting point, your **hypothesis**. An hypothesis is a possible answer to, or an explanation of, a question. It is a statement which can be proved or disproved by collecting and using relevant data.

In the comic strip the question asked was 'Who can afford to advertise on TV?' – and the hypothesis which was formed from this question was 'Only big firms advertise on TV'. The detective's question was 'Who dunnit? – and the hypothesis was 'The butler pinched the silver'.

Exercise 2

Write down an hypothesis in response to each of the following questions:
Are manufacturing firms always companies?
Do corner shops have higher prices than supermarkets?
Are trade unions only interested in wage rates?

Compare your hypotheses with someone else. Are they the same? Can more than one hypothesis be formed from the same question?

You'll probably find that someone in the class has suggested the opposite hypothesis to you. It doesn't really matter whether your hypothesis is right or wrong, it's the process that you go through to prove or disprove which is important. Think about the detective – it doesn't matter that the butler didn't pinch the silver because while the detective was collecting information to prove that the butler was guilty, he discovered that the gardener had stolen the silver so he used the information to prove the butler innocent and the gardener guilty! The same thing applies to your coursework, if you find that your original hypothesis or suggestion was not quite right, then you'll still have learned a lot from your investigations. For example, if William finds during his investigations that small firms advertise on TV as well as big firms he'll know the reasons why, and he'll probably have become quite the expert on TV advertising!

If you had difficulty with Exercise 2 you could try a different approach. One of the easiest ways of developing an hypothesis is to simply answer YES or NO to the question. The answer YES to the first question in Exercise 2 will produce the hypothesis – Manufacturing firms are always companies'. The answer NO will lead to the following hypotheses – 'Manufacturing firms are never companies'; 'Manufacturing firms are not always companies'. Now try this approach with the other questions in Exercise 2.

A DEFECTIVE DETECTIVE

There is not much point in trying to test an hypothesis you know, or are pretty sure, is not true. The defective detective in the cartoon thinks that manufacturing firms are always sole traders. This is not very realistic. So use what you know, what you've read, what you've learned from teachers to produce a reasonable hypothesis – one you think is true. You'll learn a lot more about this in the next chapter.

Now that you have a starting point, and realise that you have at least the minimum requirements for coursework, you should be ready to go ... No? ... You're still not convinced? ... Why not check the stars? ...

Capricorn
December 22 to January 20

Those born under Capricorn have a flair for research and will happily tackle very ambitious projects.

Pisces
February 19 to March 20

Pisceans, being very creative, will fish around for fascinating and unusual topics.

Aquarius
January 21 to February 18

Aquarians just love springing surprises – their coursework will be imaginative and entertaining.

Aries
March 21 to April 19

Most Arians have a no-nonsense approach and will probably produce a very well-researched project.

Taurus
April 20 to May 20

Taureans will not rush in but will take their time to methodically check out all the details.

Virgo
August 23 to September 22

Virgoans are quite clinical and will have no hesitation in throwing out irrelevant material.

Gemini
May 21 to June 21

Geminians have a talent for communicating – their work will be amusing and very readable.

Libra
September 23 to October 23

Librans always like to play safe and will only use data which has been thoroughly researched.

Cancer
June 22 to July 22

Cancerians have the knack of being in the right place at the right time – they'll have the 'hot tips'.

Scorpio
October 24 to November 22

Most Scorpios are ruthless and are capable of following enquiries relentlessly.

Leo
July 23 to August 22

Most Leos are good leaders and will confidently tackle assignments in a very grand way.

Sagittarius
November 23 to December 21

Sagittarians are naturally curious and ask lots of questions – they're natural detectives.

You should now be convinced that you can do coursework – after all it's in the stars!

Exercise 3

Use the star guide to help you to choose the members of working groups. Which star signs would you choose for a group of four members? Why?

---

3 Choosing your investigation

... BUT WHICH DIRECTION TO TAKE CAN BE A PROBLEM...

You're still with us – good! The next obstacle is choosing a topic to investigate. It's best if you develop your own ideas but if the exercises in this chapter are completed, then the ideas you collect could be used or stored in a **resource bank**. You could then draw ideas from this bank for your coursework.

Where do the ideas come from?

– course content so far

> **Exercise 1**
>
> . . . look back through the assignments and study notes you've done since you started the course. Make a list of topics or facts which have caught your interest. Now form a hypothesis for each item on your list.
>
> (Hint – this kind of task is often easier when you work in pairs or groups)

– other courses you may be following

. . . don't limit yourself to your experience gained from Business Studies or Commerce courses – you could widen your horizons and use your Geographical knowledge or even branch out into Biology.

Kate and Jane are studying Food and Nutrition as one of their options. During their course they noticed that wholemeal bread was more expensive than white bread. They were considering the question – 'Are all "healthy" foods more expensive than "ordinary"

12

foods?' – when their Business Studies teacher set a coursework assignment. Kate and Jane immediately saw this as an opportunity to follow an interest and decided to investigate the 'health food business'.

Their hypothesis was **Health foods cost more because the production is small scale**.

Exercise 2

How many different hypotheses can you form based on the topic of 'health food'?

– books

. . . have a look through your textbooks. You'll be looking at them in a rather different way – for coursework ideas rather than taking notes, revising or preparing for essays. Read the parts that interest you, look at the pictures and diagrams. You could look through reference books in the same way. Even novels can inspire ideas – *Murder on the Orient Express* by Agatha Christie might inspire an investigation into the market for unusual holidays.

– interests and hobbies

. . . can be a good source of ideas. Most people are interested in a sport or hobby which they like to talk or read about. Coursework can let you pursue your interest **in school time**!

> Roy was really keen on his local football team which played in the Fourth Division. Unfortunately the Rovers seemed to be having constant financial problems. The Supporters' Club came up with the idea that a weekly draw would help solve the problem by providing a regular source of income. Roy's dad said that it was a stupid idea and suggested selling players to raise funds. Roy was determined to prove his dad wrong and started to investigate the different ways by which the club could raise money. It occurred to him that he could do this research as a piece of coursework and used the hypothesis **Weekly draws are a good source of regular income**.

Exercise 3

Make a list of your group's interests and hobbies and suggest an investigation which could be based on each one.

– newspapers and magazines

. . . often carry headlines or articles which spark ideas. This is especially the case if the issue concerned is controversial, for example if a local authority decides to make a town centre 'pedestrians only'. There should be good scope for investigation as lots of people and organisations will be airing their views. Just look at the headlines from one issue of a local evening newspaper along with some suggested ideas for investigation.

Nappies firm plans to create 100 jobs

CONSETT is poised for a jobs boost with the news that a disposable nappies firm has attracted huge investments worth more than £3m only two years after it was launched.

What has attracted this firm to Consett?

Bakery firm fined £200

A MAN discovered a fly in a bread roll just as he was about to take a bite out of it.

Is cleanliness and hygiene a problem in food manufacture?

Rise is in line with inflation

RATEPAYERS in South Tyneside will have to find an average 3°

What effect does an increase in the price of raw materials have on manufacturers?

Warning on City rates

AS ratepayers in Newcastle today looked forward to a seven per cent cut in their bills, signs the G

However, he told the council budget meeting that an extra £20m will be needed next year to keep

reduction of 7.1 per cent for householders and 6.8 per cent for others.

Are the high city rates forcing firms to move out into the lower rated suburbs?

14

SUPERVISOR
(DAYS) c£9,750 pa

A new position for a Supervisor to work as part of the management team with a specific brief to plan, monitor and maintain the quality of service which our customers expect.

The successful applicant will have worked effectively in supervision, administration and customer liaison in a fast-moving service industry and will have the motivation, personal skills and the flexibility to make an impact. A current driving licence is essential.

JUNIOR SUPERVISOR
(NIGHTS) £8,500 pa

The Junior Supervisor will assist Night Supervision by ensuring effective administration of planning and control procedures, using computerised systems.

We are looking for a young person aged 18-25, educated to 'O' level or equivalent, who is seeking a first step to his/her career in management. Appropriate formal training will be provided.

We offer an attractive range of benefits and considerable career opportunity for the right candidates.

Please apply giving full details of your education, career and current salary to:-

Why do some people earn more than others?

HMS
RECRUITMENT
FINANCIAL ACCOUNTANT
c. £18,000 plus generous package
Our client a leading holding company with diversified interests in retail and manufacturing markets currently enjoying a

Join the **Quality** team at Nissan
Vehicle & Parts Evaluation
£7,400 p.a.

Exercise 3

Using a copy of a local newspaper, put together ideas like the ones illustrated.

– competitions

... can get you started. Every year firms and other organisations invite schools and colleges to enter local and national competitions which involve research of some kind. For example, 'Statistics Prize' which is an annual competition run by the Centre for Statistical Education. In 1985/86 there were entries covering topics such as transport, market and product research – each one suitable for a Business Studies or Commerce research project. Entering a competition could add fun to your coursework assignments as well as an incentive – ie THE PRIZE!

– enterprise schemes

... such as mini-enterprise can be used as the basis for coursework. Setting up the enterprise scheme – the actual planning and organisation could be an assignment. Any market research, publicity, production and financial systems can be used in assignments. This type of coursework will probably not involve an hypothesis so you must be careful about your presentation – but more about this later.

– work experience

... may give you a unique opportunity to investigate an issue such as health and safety, the internal structure of the firm or even storage arrangements!

> Julie and Lorraine have part time jobs in different local hairdressers. The owners of the firms, although they are not arch-enemies, are in competition with each other. The firm where Julie works was planning an advertising campaign and the girls wanted to investigate the success – or lack of success! – of the campaign. Would one firm gain at the expense of the other? The girls were in a position where they could gain 'inside information' which made their research interesting, relevant and accurate.

– contacts

... you could have an 'informer'! Your mum/dad/girl-friend/uncle/ grandma etc may be able to give you ideas from their experience at work. And if your contact owns the business . . . well the possibilities could be endless! But remember, if you solve any of their business problems, don't forget to charge a consultancy fee!

Got an idea? Can it be done?

When you've chosen your investigation you need to make sure that you haven't set yourself an impossible task. You need to test your idea.

- Is it possible for **me** to collect information?

Make sure that collecting information is not too expensive

- Is there enough information available?

  Choose a topic which can be investigated. For example, you'll not get very far trying to investigate the effect of a heatwave on ice cream sales if you choose a heatwave in 1878, or even 1976!

- Is the information relevant to Business Studies/Commerce?

  Your hobby is cycling and you investigate a firm which manufactures racing cycles. Don't collect a lot of information on 'gearing ratios' or 'saddle shapes' or lots of colourful pictures of latest models **unless they are relevant**.

- Am I really interested in this topic?

  If you have chosen a topic just because your friend did then your research is probably doomed to failure because you'll become bored and lose interest.

- Will this hypothesis cramp my style?

Don't worry if you need to change your hypothesis because your research does not go exactly to plan – but **do not** change it without first discussing any problems with your teacher.

Sometimes it is better to start research without an hypothesis. For example, you think that you're interested in the effects that consumer protection laws have on a local sweet manufacturer – but you're not sure whether you really fancy the idea. You could carry out a general investigation, possibly by spending a day at the factory just observing what is happening and talking with the people who work there. If this type of investigation appeals then you could form an hypothesis. Another situation where an hypothesis may not be needed is when your research is based on practical experience, such as an enterprise project. It may be easier to use your experience gained from the project to highlight problems and situations after they have happened – use hindsight (looking back) to help your analysis!

- Does the teacher approve?

  This is important because your coursework could be part of a GCSE assessment and the teacher will know whether your intended research project will be acceptable to the examining board. Your teacher will also be able to give advice on whether a visit to a firm is necessary or if you can find the information from another source. If you do need to visit a firm you will probably need help to make arrangements. Use your teacher as a **resource** to help you to 'cut corners' – don't turn your coursework into an endurance test!

Collecting the evidence

Introduction

Seeking information is a major part of any investigation and needs to be planned carefully. To 'find clues' you need to know what you are looking for – even if you only have a vague idea!

> When Kate and Jane started their investigation into the reasons why health foods are more expensive than other types of food, they listed the kind of information they thought would be needed (see pages 12–13).
>
> – the prices of health foods and 'ordinary' foods;
> – which firms produce health foods;
> – the methods of production used by the firms.

The information needed will decide the way in which it should be collected.

There are two sources of information.

- **Primary Sources** – this is first-hand information which you collect for yourself using different survey techniques.

- **Secondary Sources** – this is second-hand information which someone else has collected and recorded.

Kate and Jane needed to use both primary and secondary sources for their investigation and this is often the case.

4 Collecting the evidence – the 'legwork'

The word 'primary' means **first** or **original** and when this is used to describe information it means that **you** have collected **new** evidence. Nobody has ever collected this information before – it's all yours!

In Business Studies and Commerce courses we need to study market research and firms which specialise in this type of work are experts in collecting evidence. When these firms are involved in collecting primary data they say that they are doing 'field research'. The main methods of doing field research are **questionnaires**, **interviews**, **observations** and **experiments** and we shall be looking at each one of these, but first 'What is the field?'

The field contains the sources of primary data – people and organisations. Usually this means getting out of the classroom and contacting the sources, although one possible exception could be if you only need to use the people in your class. Therefore, if you want to use primary data you've got to be prepared to do the 'legwork' – but it will be worth it because you'll collect exactly the kind of information you need, probably enjoy doing it and develop some very useful research skills which you can use in other subjects.

Questionnaires

With many people the first word that comes to mind when talking about research is 'questionnaire' – but what is a questionnaire?

... IN ITS BROADEST SENSE... A QUESTIONNAIRE IS A LIST OF QUESTIONS!

Right again, Dick! but we research detectives need to know more than this . . . a questionnaire is a list of questions which will be used to seek original information from primary sources. And because each piece of research is different, each questionnaire will have to be specially designed.

If you are going to be designing questionnaires you need to have some further information. There are two types of questionnaire:

- the do-it-yourself type where the **questionnaire** is taken or posted to the person who then reads the questions, fills in their own answers and sends it back; and
- the **structured interview** where the interviewer visits or telephones the person, reads the questions out and writes down their answers.

Your first decision will be to choose which method to use, and to do this you need to consider the advantages and disadvantages of each method.

	Advantages	Disadvantages
Questionnaire	• a large number of people can be questioned • the person has time to think about their answers	• possibility of not getting many questionnaires back • you cannot explain the questions to the person
Structured interview	• the interviewer can explain the questions and give more detail if needed	• the interviewer can affect the answers, eg older people might not take students very seriously

---

Exercise 1

In each of the following situations advise the researcher on whether to use a questionnaire or a structured interview. Give reasons for your advice.

'I need to ask as many people as possible which brand of coffee they prefer.'

'I want to know if local people think the town needs more car parking space and, if they do, where they think it should be provided.'

'I want to know just what people look for when they buy a video recorder – and I want thoughtful answers!'

'I need to know the **exact** age of the person answering my questions about TV advertisements.'

Questionnaires and structured interviews both use two types of questions.

– Closed questions where the person has to choose between alternatives, for example

Tick the appropriate box:

What is your usual method of transport to work?

CAR ☐ BUS ☐ TRAIN ☐ TAXI ☐

– Open questions where the person can give more detail about their opinions, for example

What is your usual method of transport to work?

Bus – but this is because I haven't saved

enough money to buy a car... but if there

was a railway station nearby ...

By looking at the two examples given you can see that the way in which the person is allowed to answer may greatly affect the type of data you collect.

The **closed** question should be used when you need to count different answers and analyse them, or when the information you are seeking is quite specific.

For example, you might want to find out how popular supermarket 'own brands' are compared to other brands. You could ask a closed question such as

Which brand of coffee do you use regularly?
(Tick the box which applies to you)

SUPERMARKET OWN BRAND ☐

NESCAFE ☐

MAXWELL HOUSE ☐

BROOKE BOND ☐

What if the person doesn't use any of these brands?

Add another alternative   OTHER (please state) _____

Using this type of question it is fairly simple to add up the results and arrive at an answer such as '20% of people buy supermarket own brand'.

You can use closed questions to seek opinions on specific matters.

For example, you might want to find out the person's opinion on 'brand loyalty'. You could ask the question

> Most people don't bother to compare the price of coffee, they just buy their usual brand.
> (Tick the box which is nearest to your view)
>
> STRONGLY AGREE ☐
>
> AGREE ☐
>
> DON'T KNOW ☐
>
> DISAGREE ☐
>
> STRONGLY DISAGREE ☐

Exercise 2

Write closed questions to find out the following:

a) the kind of magazines your friend buys;
b) what make of car your friends' parents own;
c) whether a school 'car wash' enterprise scheme would be used by staff.

Test questions (a) and (b) in the class, and change them where necessary. Test question (c) among the staff in your school – this could be **real** market research.

Sometimes the information you're looking for is quite general. You may not be familiar with all the alternatives so you need to ask an **open** question.

For example, you are investigating the reason for the success of a corner shop. You know the 'textbook' reasons, but you're not convinced so you ask the question:

'Why do you use P Pod's shop?'

Your research reveals that an important reason for success is that P Pod lets the gardeners from the local allotment sell their surplus produce in his shop. Now you didn't know this. If you'd asked a closed question, you would not have put this as one of the alternative answers. This example shows how open questions can sometimes produce more accurate information.

Open questions are also useful if you want people's views and opinions. Suppose you want to discover why people prefer a particular brand of lager. It's often better to let them give their own answers rather than choose between alternatives which you have given. An open question allows them to say exactly what they mean in their own way.

Most questionnaires contain both closed and open questions because researchers will need both specific information – facts and figures – and people's views and opinions.

Exercise 3

Look at the extract from a questionnaire (on pages 25 and 26) which sought information about people's spending patterns. What kind of problems do you think the researcher could meet using this questionnaire? Give reasons for your answers.

PATTERNS OF SPENDING
SECTION A

1 Have you bought any shoes in Blyth during the last six months?

   YES ☐ NO ☐

2 Did you buy the shoes from:

   SHOEFAYRE ☐   STAR MARKET ☐   Please tick

   CO-OP ☐   ROBSONS ☐

   CURTESS ☐   PAIGES ☐

   STAR SHOES ☐   Others ....

3 Did you buy shoes for:

   SCHOOL ☐   LEISURE ☐   Please tick

   WORK ☐   SPECIAL OCCASIONS ☐

                        Others ....

4 Were the shoes in a sale?

   YES ☐ NO ☐

5 Did the shop have a wide variety of shoes for all occasions?

   YES ☐ NO ☐

(continued on page 26)

25

SECTION B   PATTERNS OF SPENDING (continued)

1 Have you bought any clothes in Blyth during the last six months?

YES ☐ NO ☐

2 Did you buy: Cross out appropriate answer

SKIRTS/TROUSERS ☐   Dorothy Perkins/Burtons/Drapers/Seconds Ahead

Others ....

BLOUSE/SHIRT ☐   Dorothy Perkins/Burtons/Drapers/Seconds Ahead

Others ....

COAT ☐   Dorothy Perkins/Burtons/Drapers/Seconds Ahead

Others ....

NIGHTWEAR ☐   Dorothy Perkins/Cooknells/Woodcocks/Co-op

Others ....

UNDERWEAR ☐   Dorothy Perkins/Cooknells/Woodcocks/Co-op

Others ....

3 Did you buy the article in a sale?

YES ☐ NO ☐

4 Did the shop have a wide variety of the article you bought?

YES ☐ NO ☐

(Wendy van Es)

Exercise 4

Suppose you want to investigate spending patterns in your town. Rewrite sections A and B using both closed and open questions.

Now that you have some basic information about questionnaires you need to choose who is going to answer your questions. Suppose you want to investigate the popularity of certain teenage magazines. Ideally you want to give a questionnaire to every teenager in Great Britain but this is just not possible. What do other investigators do? The BBC compiles the Top Twenty using the same population that you are interested in, how do they manage? How do market researchers discover if there is a market among teenagers for a new soft drink? They choose a smaller number of teenagers. This smaller number is called a **sample**.

The sample should represent the population as a whole – it should be a cross-section. This allows you to say that the results you obtain from your sample probably apply to the whole of the population. For example, if most of the sample said they liked Cherry Coke, then you could say 'most teenagers in Great Britain like Cherry Coke' because your sample results will 'back up' your statement.

Choosing a representative sample

You must take care when choosing a sample because your results will be affected by the kind of people you choose.

Example Population: the people who use P Pod's shop
Suggested method of sampling: QUOTA SAMPLE

- Observe the shop at different times of the day and on different days of the week.

- Note the age, sex and ethnic background of the shoppers.

- Your sample should include the same proportion of people using the shop, eg if 20% of shoppers are young boys, then 20% of your sample should be young boys.

Example Population: members of a local athletics club
Suggested method of sampling: STRATIFIED RANDOM SAMPLE

- Ask permission to look at a list of members of the club. A list of names from which you can choose your sample is called a SAMPLING FRAME.

- Make separate lists of male and female members so that you can make sure the sample is representative.
- Give each name on the lists a number, eg 1–200.
- Choose a RANDOM sample from each list. A random sample is one which is based on pure chance. Ask your Maths teacher for a list of random numbers and simply choose as many numbers as you want. If you don't want to use random numbers you can choose every third, fourth, or whatever, number on the lists. This is known as SYSTEMATIC sampling.
- The 'lucky numbers' are given a questionnaire.

Exercise 5

1) Why would **stratified random sampling** be unsuitable when choosing a sample of people using P Pod's shop?
2) How could **systematic sampling** be used to choose a sample of these shoppers?
3) **Quota sampling** has not worked very well and the sample of shoppers is not very representative. How could this have happened? What do you think went wrong?
4) Show how successful you think **quota sampling** could be when choosing a sample from the members of the athletics club.

How big should the sample be?

Your sample shouldn't be so big that you cannot manage to collect the data, but it should be big enough to accurately represent the population. A sample of 10 out of a population of 1000 will probably not be very representative – even if you choose very carefully – but 10 out of a population of 50 could be fairly representative. The size of the population will affect your sample size – always remember to include an explanation of your choice of sample and any problems you had so that your results can be interpreted in a realistic way.

Exercise 6

You want to give a questionnaire to a sample of 50 pupils at your school to help the school committee to decide whether or not to install a drinks machine.

1) What could you use as a sampling frame?
2) How could you make sure that equal numbers of pupils from each year group were included in the sample?

Sorting the results

When the interviews are finished and the questionnaires have been returned, you will need to collect the evidence together so that you can work with it easily.

Answers to open questions could be collected together so that you can use them for quotations and references – they provide good 'back-up'. They also provide entertaining quotations to brighten up your report, eg

'This brand of coffee tastes like tea.'

'No wonder they call it Gold Blend, the price they charge.'

'It's a waste of time asking which brand of coffee I prefer. I can't stand the stuff'.

An easy way to count answers is to follow this method

- Give each questionnaire a number – to make sure that you don't count someone's answers twice.

- Give each question a number – this helps you to compare different answers to the same question.

- Give each alternative answer a number – this is known as a 'code' and helps when counting.

By using this method you can transfer all the information on to a single chart which is much easier to work with. See the chart on page 30.

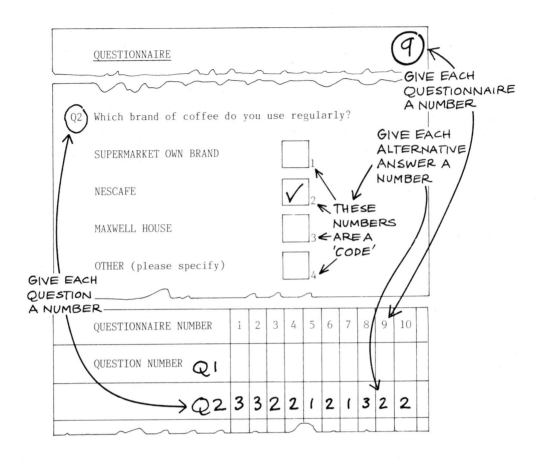

But what does this mean? We need to count the answers to see –

SUPERMARKET OWN BRAND (alternative 1) – 2 out of 10 users.
NESCAFE (alternative 2) – 5 out of 10 users.
MAXWELL HOUSE (alternative 3) – 3 out of 10 users.
OTHER BRANDS (alternative 4) – no users.

You can now make a statement about the results, for example,

Half the sample use Nescafe.
20% of the sample use supermarket own brand.
No-one in the sample uses any other brand than those stated.

. . . or you might want to give the results in the form of a chart or graph . . .

30

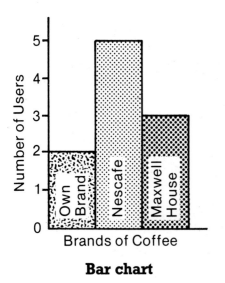

Bar chart

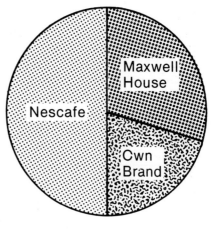

Pie chart

Exercise 7

Results can sometimes be presented in a **line graph**.

Louise had been investigating depreciation of cars and these are some of her results.

AGE OF CAR	AVERAGE PRICE	
	FORD FIESTA 1.1 L	AUSTIN METRO 1.0 L
New	£4995	£4850
1 year	£3975	£3825
2 years	£3350	£3225
3 years	£2825	£2650
4 years	£2225	£2025
5 years	£2000	£2000

Show these results on a graph – use a different colour for each car.

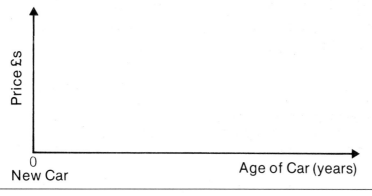

Standard procedure: questionnaires

Activity	Before proceeding
DECIDE to use a questionnaire	– what are you trying to find out? – is this the **best** way? – who will you ask?
DRAFT the questionnaire in rough	– is there a reason for each question? (too many questions put people off) – are the questions clear and simple? – should the questions be closed or open? – do you need to 'code' closed questions?
Have a DUMMY-RUN among friends/relatives	– do the questions work? – do any questions need to be changed? – do you need to add any questions?

DUPLICATE questionnaires	– how many copies do you need?
	– if you want to question the general public, have you checked with your teacher?
	– have you included
	    ● your name
	    ● your school or college
	    ● the course to which the questionnaire relates
	    ● the research topic
	    ● that all answers will be confidential?
	    (people like to know these things)

DATA COLLECTION	**questionnaires** – has everybody in the sample received a copy? – do they know how to fill it in? – have you made arrangements to collect completed questionnaires? **structured interviews** – have you got a pen and something to lean on? – have you practised reading the questions so you can ask everybody in the same way? – have you arranged a suitable place for the interview?
DISPLAY results	– have you included only relevant evidence? – did you consider different ways of presenting results before deciding? – have you included quotations?

DRAW CONCLUSIONS	– have you written up your results as soon as possible stating
	    ● why you used this method
	    ● how you chose the sample
	    ● any unusual results
	    ● any problems you met
	    ● any mistakes you made
	    ● any changes you would make if you did it again?

Interviews

There are two types of interviews

- the **structured interview** which is based on a standard questionnaire, and

- the **'in-depth'** interview which uses more general questions and tends to be more like a 'chat' so that the person answering can give more detailed answers.

Structured interviews are used when the researcher is seeking quite specific information from a large number of people.

In-depth interviews are used when the researcher is seeking general information from individuals who may be experts or who may have valuable opinions or interesting points of view.

Exercise 9

In each of the following situations advise the researcher whether to use a structured or in-depth interview. State the advantages the researcher will gain by following your advice.

'I want to know how often people buy records and what kind they buy.'

'I want to investigate how consumer protection laws affect retailers, but I'm not sure what questions to ask.'

'I want to investigate the effect that last year's increase in membership fees had on the number of people joining the golf club.'

'I want to investigate the effect that the proposed increase in membership fees may have on existing members of the golf club.'

'I need to know exactly what happened to cause the strike.'

'I should like to know how the two part-time mechanics actually feel about job sharing.'

Sorting the results

Not all the information gained from an interview will be useful. It could be either inaccurate or irrelevant or both!

The information could be inaccurate due to

- 'leading questions' which cause the person to tell you what they think you want to hear, for example

  'Disposable nappies are well worth the extra money, aren't they?'

- the person may be embarrassed by the question, for example

  'Do you use a laxative?'

- the reliability of the person's knowledge, for example

  'But Grandma, are you really sure that washing up liquid had a nicer smell when you were young?'

- the ambitions of the person answering, as shown in the cartoon.

Some of the information collected could be irrelevant. This would be especially true if you've been conducting an in-depth interview and the person has been 'telling you all they know'. For example, if you've interviewed the chemist in charge of producing biological soap powder, you should not include all the information about production – you may only need to include the facts about what makes mass production possible.

Standard procedure: interviews

Activity	Before proceeding
CONSIDER the benefits	– what are you trying to find out? – is this the **best** way?
CONTACT the people involved	– who will you ask? – how many people do you need to interview? – have you asked permission for the interview? – have you explained who you are and what you are doing?
CHECK your planning	– have you worked out a plan? – is your questionnaire ready for structured interviews? – have you a list of questions to cover basic information for in-depth interviews? – how will you encourage the person to talk to you? – how will you collect the information?

CONFIRM the arrangements	– is the proposed time convenient?
	– is the place suitable?
	– does the person need a copy of the questions before the interview to collect information?
	– are you using a cassette recorder?
	    ● does it have good batteries
	    ● have you a blank cassette
	    ● do you know how it works?

Continued overleaf.

Standard procedure: interviews (continued)

Activity	Before proceeding
CONDUCT the interview	– will you remember to introduce yourself? – can you be friendly, but serious? – will you listen carefully and not allow note making /recording to interrupt? – can you keep to the point? – can you follow interesting leads? – will you remember to say 'thank you' at the end?

COPY up your results	– have you written up as soon as possible in case you cannot understand your notes?
	– did you sort the information and reject the irrelevant parts?
	– have you made a list of quotations?
	– does your analysis include
	    ● why you used this method
	    ● how you planned the interview
	    ● any problems
	    ● any mistakes
	    ● how useful the interview was
	    ● any changes you would make if you did it again?

Exercise 10

Go through the STANDARD PROCEDURE and make a list of points you need to remember when using an interview as a research method.

Agree your list with the rest of the group and make a poster headed 'DOs and DON'Ts of interviews'.

Practise your interviewing techniques.

Exercise 11

Plan and conduct an in-depth interview with someone in your class on one of the following:

shopping in hypermarkets;
shops being open on Sundays;
pubs being open all day.

Take notes and write up the results of the interview, adding your own comments where you think necessary.

Observation

Observation involves looking and listening very carefully in order to discover information. There are two types of observation.

- **Direct observation** is when the researcher can watch what is happening without joining in the activity. For example, a researcher who observes employees in a supermarket, just like a bird watcher observes birds.

- **Participant observation** is when the researcher deliberately joins in with the activities of a group while observing them. For example, a researcher working in a supermarket observing employees.

When would observation be useful?

- Many people don't think about what they do – they just do it! So if you were to ask a person to describe their working day they would probably miss out the things they do without thinking, such as chatting to a friend, or combing their hair! By using direct observation you could find out **exactly** how that worker spends their working day.

Direct observation is very important in organisations where work study specialists observe how a job is performed. They use the information to calculate prices and wage rates, or simply to improve efficiency. You could study a worker or organisation in the same way as part of an investigation.

- You might want to see how a person's behaviour changes under different circumstances. In answering a questionnaire lots of people might say that they are not affected by advertising. You could use direct observation to watch shoppers' reactions to an in-store demonstration which encourages sampling of chocolate biscuits. Many people who said they were not affected by advertising may well buy a packet of the chocolate biscuits!

- Sometimes the people involved may be unable or unwilling to give interviews or answer questionnaires. In these situations observation could be the only way of finding out information. You might want to find out how many fruit pastilles are eaten by packers in a sweet factory. The packers probably don't know how many they eat – and if they did probably would not tell!

It is unlikely that you would have enough time to become a member of a new group but you could do some participant observation in a group or situation with which you already have contact. If you have a part-time job you could observe the attitudes of workers to safety or security rules. You could assess how effective the channels of communication are within a firm because, as an employee, you will often be on the receiving end!

Observe the effectiveness of communication channels.

Exercise 12

CHRIS AND THE CAR PARK SURVEY

Shoppers were complaining that people who worked in the town were filling the two small car parks and the shoppers could not find spaces. The local council was considering introducing charges for parking and these would make it very expensive to leave a car all day.

Chris did not believe that the parking spaces were taken by workers and used observation to find out.

He drew a map of one car park showing the parking spaces. On market day, Chris went to the car park at 8 am and wrote down the registration numbers of the cars parked. At 9 am he went around the car park and noted any changes. Chris continued making observations right through the day until 6 pm.

1) Why do you think Chris decided to use observation?
2) Why did he choose a market day?
3) What problems do you think Chris might have met?
4) In what ways could Chris present his results?
5) Suppose Chris found that workers do park their cars all day. What conclusions can Chris draw?

Standard procedure: observation

Activity	Before proceeding
STUDY the benefits	– what are you trying to find out? – is observation possible? – is this the **best** way of seeking the information?
SPEAK to anyone involved	– have you made arrangements? – do you need permission? – how long will it take?

SET out headings	– do you know exactly what you're looking for?
	– have you made suitable headings, such as SHOP ASSISTANT'S TIME SPENT
	    ● talking to customers
	    ● talking on telephone
	    ● walking around
	    ● tidying shelves?

SEE what there is to see	– have you got a clear idea what you're looking for? – can you make notes? ● if you can't how will you remember what you see? – can you manage to stay out of people's way?
SORT out your evidence	– have you written up your results as soon as possible? – have you worked out what you've discovered? – have you found a suitable method of presentation? (see 'questionnaires' page 31)

SUM up your findings	– does your analysis include
	    ● why you used this method
	    ● how you planned it
	    ● any problems you met
	    ● any mistakes you made
	    ● any changes you would make if you did it again?

Experiments

Sometimes it is possible to include experiments as a method of collecting information. Experiments involve discovering the effect of one thing on another. In Business Studies or Commerce we would use experiments to test a person's reaction to a product.

When would experiments be useful?

● If you were investigating brand loyalty

    – you could test to see if people know the difference between 'own brand' and 'branded' products such as coffee.

- If you were investigating the influence of packaging on sales
  - wrap the same product, eg a chocolate bar, in different ways and ask a sample of people which product they would buy.
- If you were investigating people's attitudes towards new or unusual products
  - invite people to sample a new product such as 'blue lemonade' and note their reactions.

Exercise 13

Design an experiment to compare the effectiveness of different methods of communication used within an organisation.

Standard procedure: experiments

Activity	Before proceeding
EXAMINE the benefits	– what are you trying to find out? – will an experiment be useful? – have you discussed using this method with your teacher?
EQUIPMENT	– have you prepared the equipment you need? – does everybody involved know what to do? – have you got permission to do the experiment? – how will you record your findings?
Do the EXPERIMENT	– have you taken care to keep the conditions the same? ● you cannot test Sainsbury v Nescafe one day and Sainsbury v Maxwell House the next.

EXPLAIN your results	– does your explanation include
	    ● why you used an experiment
	    ● how you planned it
	    ● any problems you met
	    ● any mistakes you made
	    ● what your results show
	    ● how the experiment could have been improved?

5 Collecting the evidence – the 'deskwork'

Not again! But he is right, you can do your research while sitting at a desk – you don't have to visit lots of people to collect the facts you need. You can use **secondary data**.

Secondary data is information which someone else has found out and you can use it. The information could have been written in a book or a newspaper, or it might be stored in a database, or it is possible that it has been recorded on audio- or videotape. Whatever the source of the data, you can 'borrow' it to help your investigation, but it must be treated with care.

General Research Warning ⚠ Careless use of SECONDARY DATA can damage your research

- The data was not collected specially for your research so you must choose carefully what you use – be selective and do not copy out huge chunks!

- Some data will be more accurate and reliable than others – government figures will probably be more reliable than an article in *The Sun*.

- Use secondary data to back up your research, to help you to make a point and **always** include your own comments on the reliability and reasons for using it.

When you look at secondary data you'll find that it comes in all sorts of shapes and forms – in words, pictures or tables; it might be in black and white or it could be coloured. Whatever it looks like, apart from gathering information, you could find lots of ideas to help you with the presentation of your research findings – so it's always worth doing some deskwork.

There are lots of different secondary sources which you could use for your research, but most of the data you use will come from **official statistics**, the **mass media**, **books** and **organisations**. We shall be looking at each one of these sources, but first – read the GENERAL RESEARCH WARNING again and remember that this warning applies to **all** secondary sources – even if they are not mentioned in this book.

Official statistics

In this instance 'official' means government and official statistics are the facts and figures which have been collected by different branches of local and national government. The government needs to collect this information so that they can plan for the future.

Exercise 1

The Department of Transport collects information on driving tests, such as the number of applications made, how many tests were taken and passed, and even compares the pass rates of males and females.

1) Why might the government need to know this information?
2) Suppose you were making a general investigation into driving schools. How could the information collected by the Department of Transport help your research?

There are many government departments which collect and publish information. Much of this information is very detailed and it is often easier to use books which contain a selection of the most interesting official statistics, unless, of course, you know **exactly** what you want.

You can find official statistics in school or college libraries or you might need to use the local reference library. No matter which library you use it is worthwhile asking for some help because there is so much information available. The people who can probably help are

- your teacher (who may even have a copy of exactly what you need!)
- your school or college librarian
- the librarian at your local reference library

or you could write to the local or national government department concerned. The list of useful addresses on pages 111–115 gives you further information on how to obtain official publications.

The following books and publications are ones which you'll probably find most useful. When you use them make sure to use the most up-to-date edition.

Social Trends This contains a wide range of statistics often showing changes over a period of time. The information is in charts and tables with some discussion of the facts.

Annual Abstract of Statistics Similar to *Social Trends* but the statistics are more detailed and there is no discussion.

Key Data Contains the most important social and economic statistics in any year.

Regional Trends A selection of the main statistics available on the various regions of the UK.

Economic Progress Report This is published every two months and contains a variety of economic information along with tables showing exchange rates, interest rates etc.

British Business Published weekly, this contains information on consumer prices, imports and consumer credit.

If you want **local** information **Small Area Statistics** taken from the government census are available for each local government ward. These include information on the age, sex, marital status and economic activity of the people in your immediate locality. You can get this information from reference libraries or by writing to your local authority.

1. Do you understand what the statistics show?

If you don't then you cannot be selective and choose carefully what you use. You need to pay special attention to the headings of tables to find out exactly what the table is telling you. The following table is from *Social Trends*, 1986.

Availability of durable goods: by socio-economic group of head of household

Great Britain   Percentages

	Profes-sional, employers, and managers		Inter-mediate non-manual		Junior non-manual		Skilled manual and own account non-prof-essional		Semi-skilled manual and personal service		Unskilled manual		All heads of household[1]		
	1979	1983	1979	1983	1979	1983	1979	1983	1979	1983	1979	1983	1979	1983	1984
Percentage of households with:															
Refrigerator[2]	96	97	95	96	93	96	92	95	88	91	82	90	92	94	94
Deep-freezer[2]	61	77	47	61	36	49	41	61	28	43	18	36	40	57	61
Washing machine	85	89	72	79	71	72	80	86	67	73	57	68	74	80	79
Tumble drier	30	42	20	30	14	22	19	29	12	21	8	14	18	28	29
Dishwasher	12	15	3	6	1	2	1	2	1	1	–	–	3	5	5
Telephone	90	95	82	88	74	81	65	76	49	63	39	53	6/	77	78
Central heating	78	83	66	75	58	66	50	61	41	50	36	49	55	64	66
Television															
Colour	79	91	66	83	66	80	71	84	55	71	44	65	66	81	83
Black and white only	18	7	28	14	30	18	27	14	42	26	50	31	31	17	14
Video recorder	··	24	··	18	··	12	··	20	··	12	··	12	··	17	24
Home computer	··	··	··	··	··	··	··	··	··	··	··	··	··	··	9

[1]Includes members of the armed forces, full-time students, people in inadequately described occupations, and all people who have never worked.

[2] Fridge-freezers are included in both Refrigerator and Deep-freezer.

Source: *Social Trends*, (1986)

Exercise 2

The questions in this exercise will help you to read the table carefully.

1) To which country does the table refer?
2) Which dates are mentioned in the table?
3) How is the information given? (£s, thousands, percentages, etc)
4) Into how many different groups have the 'heads of household' been divided?
5) How many different kinds of durable goods are listed?
6) What is the original source of the data?

Now that you've read the table do you know what it shows? The questions in Exercise 3 will help you to understand what the table is 'saying'.

Exercise 3

1) How many households had a tumble drier in 1984?
2) 76% of certain households had a telephone in 1983 – which type of households?
3) Which durable goods do 'Unskilled Manual' households seem not to buy?
4) What was the general increase in households owning colour televisions? (Describe the trend from 1979).
5) Which household durable has shown the greatest increase in popularity?

---

2. Do you know what the figures actually mean?

You cannot use statistics without drawing some conclusions about what they show. The statistics themselves will be the results of someone else's investigation and experienced detectives know that the figures 'don't speak for themselves', they could be inaccurate or unreliable. Exercise 4 lets you practise interpretation skills using the same table from *Social Trends*.

3. Are you sure the figures are reliable?

Just because the statistics are 'official' it doesn't mean that they are totally reliable. There are different ways of measuring things, for example, unemployment. Official statistics are based on the number of people who register as being unemployed. But there are lots of people who do not register because they are not entitled to unemployment benefit. They are unemployed but the government does not count them in the official unemployment figures. Until you know what the figures 'really mean', official statistics can be very misleading. This is shown in the graph and article on page 48.

Exercise 4

'Today, 79% of households own a washing machine.'

'In 1984 there were no households owning a fridge-freezer.'

'Video recorders were invented in 1983.'

'Members of the armed forces, students, people with strange occupations and layabouts are the only people who own home computers.'

'Bosses have more consumer durables than the workers.'

- For each of the statements above –

  a) state whether you agree or disagree
  b) use data from the table to support your answers to (a)

- Give **three** reasons why some data in the table might be unreliable. For example, some people might not own up to having a TV because they don't have a licence.

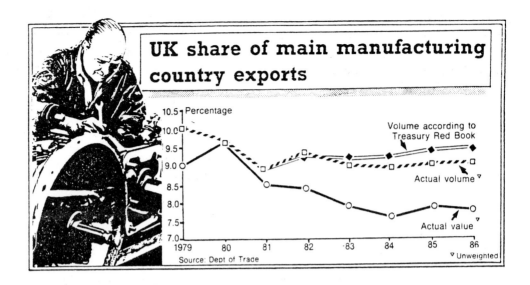

UK share of main manufacturing country exports

Percentage

Volume according to Treasury Red Book

Actual volume ▽

Actual value ▽

1979 80 81 82 ·83 84 85 86

Source: Dept of Trade

▽ Unweighted

ONE OF the many claims made by the Government in the run up to the election is that the long term decline in the UK's share of world trade in manufactured goods has been reversed. According to the Government, this is evidence of a streamlined manufacturing sector winning back lost markets. *What we find however, is that this claim is based on a selective choice and somewhat misleading use of statistics.*

It is clear that the new way of presenting the facts portrays our export performance in a more favourable light. Using its new definition, the Government has been able to claim that export share has been on an upward trend since 1981 and that we will soon return to 1980 levels. In contrast, the old definition shows our export share little different from the all time low of 1981.

Exercise 5

1) Which year does the 'Volume according to Treasury Red Book' start to differ from 'Actual volume'?
2) The difference is caused by a change in definition of exports. Why do the writers of this article think the government changed the definition?

(Notice the presentation of the graph – you might be able to use this idea!)

4. Do the statistics improve your case?

Don't use statistics unless they back up your case, or help to emphasise a point, or at least add **something** to your work. Suppose you were investigating the effect of 'interest-free' credit as a technique for marketing cars (durable goods). You could use official statistics to

- provide background information for use in an introduction

Example: Use the information in the chart to show how much of their income people spend on durables – according to these statistics in 1985 consumers spent £2.1 bn.

Summary personal sector accounts

	1985	£ billion
	Total personal income	**303.9**
less	Deductions from income	64.1
equals	**Total personal disposable income**	**239.8**
less	Consumers' expenditure:	
	non-durable goods and services	192.2
	durable goods	21.0
equals	**Personal sector saving**	**26.6**
	Personal sector saving ratio	**11.1%**

Source: *Economic Progress Report* No. 187, Nov–Dec 1986

- compare your findings to official figures

  Example: You find that people with high incomes spend a greater proportion of their income on buying cars. There is a section in *Social Trends* which gives information on this – households with an income of less than £100 spent 8%, whereas households with an income of more than £300 spent nearly 18%.

- give a national picture when your research is local

  Example: Your research may have been carried out in a fairly rich part of the country where 75% of households have the use of a car – nationally only 44% of households have regular use of a car.

- compare different areas

  Example: After discovering the difference in the previous example you could explain the reasons by using comparative income levels using *Regional Trends*.

- give a picture over time

  Example: You might want to show that constantly high interest rates mean 'interest-free' credit is attractive to customers. You could use information from *Economic Progress Report* to show the trend.

- comment on people's attitudes

  Example: In your research people said that they thought more people in Japan owned cars than in Britain. In fact, in 1983 there were only 221 cars per 1000 Japanese, compared to 312 cars per 1000 Britons – you could comment on this.

Only 221 cars per 1000 Japanese compared to 312 cars per 1000 Britons

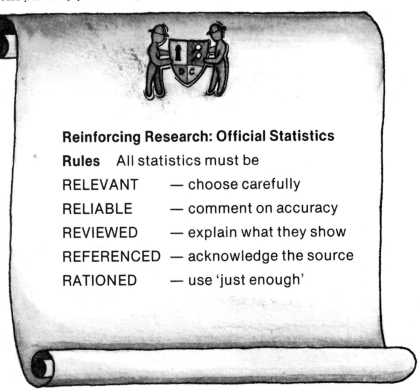

Reinforcing Research: Official Statistics

Rules   All statistics must be

RELEVANT   — choose carefully

RELIABLE   — comment on accuracy

REVIEWED   — explain what they show

REFERENCED   — acknowledge the source

RATIONED   — use 'just enough'

Mass media

The word **media** is used to describe the ways that information is communicated: in this instance, **mass** means a very large amount – so we can safely say that the **mass media** are the ways of communicating information to a very large number of people!

There are many different ways of communicating information. However the media you will probably find most useful are newspapers and magazines. You might also find radio and television helpful. With so many different kinds of newspapers and magazines around you might not know where to begin to look for information. A general guide would be to rely on the mass media only when you have a clear idea what you are looking for but otherwise don't **expect** to find 'the perfect article'. Because finding information is so much of a gamble, it's a good idea to always keep a look out for articles and programmes, and what you don't use you can store in a resource bank – or share with a friend!

● Newspapers come in lots of varieties. They can be

  – local or national
  – daily or weekly
  – 'quality', eg *The Daily Telegraph*
    'popular', eg *The Daily Mirror*
    'alternative', eg *The Morning Star*

Look at the business or money pages for possible articles and up-to-date figures on exchange rates or share prices.

● Magazines also come in lots of varieties. They can be

  – weekly, monthly or quarterly;
  – for a mixed readership, eg *The Listener* or one type of reader, eg *Woman's Own*
  – for general interest, eg *Colour Supplements* or for specialist interest, eg *The Investor*

51

Your choice of magazine will depend upon the kind of information you're seeking. If it is general you'll just have to take your chance; for financial information use specialist magazines such as *The Economist*. Monthly magazines might have an index of the topics covered during the year – this is usually in the December issue. If you go to your local library, there will probably be back copies of the magazine – and a librarian to help you!

- Television and Radio can be

  - local or national
  - BBC or commercial

It's worth watching regular business and consumer programmes such as *The Money Programme* or *That's Life* because obviously there's a greater chance of finding 'something useful'. Some documentaries such as *World in Action* or *QED* could be useful, and there's often useful material on Radio 4 – save time by using the TV and radio programme guides to find out what the programmes are about.

SPECIAL RESEARCH WARNING   MASS MEDIA

1. Is the information reliable?

Journalists do not simply report 'facts'. They try to make their article or programme exciting and interesting to their audience. You need to be careful and read the article with the thought that the 'real facts' could be distorted by someone's point of view. For example, a female journalist who supports women's lib will treat the topic 'Women in Management' quite differently to a journalist who is a male chauvinist! It doesn't mean that you cannot use quotes from the article but include your own comment,

> '. . . of course this information might be biased as it was reported by . . .'

2. Have you been selective?

Remember that the data is supposed to improve **your** case. It hasn't been collected or written specially for you so don't copy out huge chunks of articles – be selective and **choose appropriate quotations**.

Exercise 6

DAILY EXPRESS Monday March 30 1987

 **EXPRESS**

The franchising industry is coming under closer scrutiny after enjoying a period of almost uncritical acclaim.

It would be surprising if that were not the case. Franchising has grown so fast in Britain in recent years that inevitably it has attracted some disreputable operators.

Also, the general euphoria surrounding the industry has tended to mask the fact that although franchising is arguably the safest way of going into business, it is not without risk.

Prospective investors should look for certain pointers.

● If a franchisor belongs to the British Franchise Association, that is a good sign. The instant framing service, Fastframe, for example, is one of the quickest growing concerns in the UK and a member of the BFA.

● Franchises owned or operated by publicly-quoted companies are also a fair bet. One such is the dry-cleaning chain, Euroclean, which is part of the Black Arrow Group. It, too, is growing quickly, and looking for new franchisees.

An increasing number of franchises now offer financial packages in partnership with one or other of the High Street banks. Given the notorious caution of bankers, their support has to be a good sign. Metro-Rod, for example, the lesser-known rival to pipe-and-drain cleaning pioneer Dyno-Rod, offers packages from £16,000 with 70 per cent finance available.

Obviously, none of these pointers excludes the others, and the more signs of financial and management stability, the better.

You are investigating franchising. Select appropriate quotes to emphasise

a) that franchising is increasing;

b) the signs that franchising is a 'good risk'.

3. Does the information improve your case?

You can use cuttings and quotations from the mass media to

- add reality to what you are saying
  - taking franchising (again!), you could use quotations from an article which compares the experience of three different people to emphasise aspects such as

Financing	**Economies**	**Control**
(Pizza Express)	(Holland & Barrett)	(The Body Shop)
of course it was difficult at first. We had to put up a lot of our own money and borrow some from the bank. It is quite frightening when you see how much you've got to borrow – it was equal to about three years' wages! But I believe you have to take a risk to get anywhere in this life. And franchising is a much smaller risk than starting up on your own, provided you pick the right franchise, that is.	"I'm not exactly in the millionaire bracket yet, but I'm not doing as badly as I might have done if I'd set up on my own. Being part of a big chain meant I could negotiate a cheaper rent, and I can often get supplies cheaper than I might have been able to otherwise. Also, I had to borrow all that money from the bank before I started, and they might not have been so willing to put that up if they didn't know they had a good chance of getting it back!	"Of course it's all changed now. These days it's much bigger and a lot better organised, so I tend to take my lead from head office a lot more than we did then. The way I see it, they have access to a lot more expertise than I do, so I might as well listen to them!

- find financial information which is up-to-date

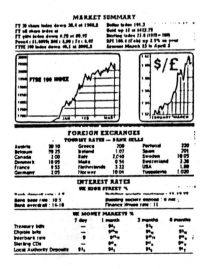

and share prices too!

- collect a range of the same type of data
  - for comparing the prices of second-hand cars, and in fact lots of other articles, a magazine such as *Exchange and Mart* will be useful.

This edition had prices for 142 Porsches – you'd be lucky to find half a dozen in the local newspaper!

- emphasise a point
  - you've already practised this in Exercise 6.

- brighten up your work
  - **one** or **two** coloured pictures, or a cartoon, might help to break up a page of writing, but don't overdo it.

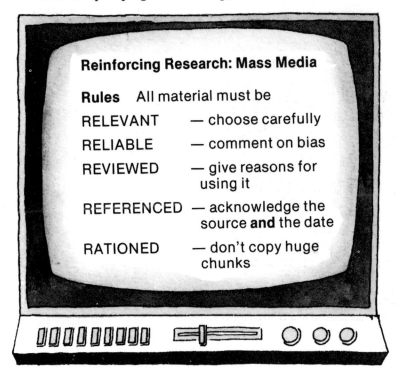

Reinforcing Research: Mass Media

Rules   All material must be

RELEVANT	— choose carefully
RELIABLE	— comment on bias
REVIEWED	— give reasons for using it
REFERENCED	— acknowledge the source **and** the date
RATIONED	— don't copy huge chunks

Books

No Dick, I'm afraid not . . . he's not very clued up when it comes to secondary data, is he? You'll probably not find any really useful information in a novel either, although you might get some 'leads' or ideas to follow up. The books which you will find helpful will be textbooks and reference books, and you might get the chance to read other researchers' reports.

- Textbooks can be found in school or college, or in your local library. Ask your teacher because there might be textbooks which you don't know about.

- Reference books need to be updated quite often and renewing them can be expensive. Because of the cost involved you'll probably find a better selection of reference books in your local library, rather than in school – but because of the wide choice you'll need to ask the librarian to help.

- Reports by other researchers are more likely to be found in polytechnic and university libraries rather than local libraries. Many of these will be complicated so unless your teacher gives you advice on which ones to use, stick to textbooks and reference books.

1. Did you choose the material carefully?

You really must remember that this information is not yours. It hasn't been collected specially for your research. You might have used Economics, Geography, History or Social Science textbooks as well as Business Studies and Commerce books, so you must only use relevant information.

2. Did you state where the information came from?

Keep a list of all the books you use and include this in your coursework. If you copy any information from the books show that it is not yours by using quotation marks.

3. Is the information reliable?

If the book you use is not about Business Studies or Commerce you will need to include a comment on what you're trying to show. You will need to look at the age of the book in case the material is out-of-date – there are still lots of textbooks which state '50' as the maximum numbers of shareholders in a private company, and '7' as the minimum for all public companies!

4. Does the data improve your case?

Don't feel that you **must** use books because sometimes they may not be relevant to your investigation. For example, if you have been conducting a survey of how people react to different flavours of ice cream you may not need to use books at all. Use books to improve your investigation and not simply to 'pad it out'.

There are several ways in which books can help...

Uses of books

There are several ways in which you can use books to help your investigation. **Textbooks** can be used for

● general investigations

> – when you first start an investigation it's a good idea to read about the topic so that you can set off in the right direction.

> Example: You might want to compare the production of electronic components by a small firm with a large firm. How do you know what are large and small firms? You'll need to use some method of measurement and a textbook will give you different ways to do this. It could be based on the number of employees, or the number of branches; the amount of profits, capital or output.

● explanations of how something works

> Example: If you are investigating the marketing of a product this diagram could help you to explain different methods of distribution, eg the difference between distributing washing machines and washing powder.

Channels of distribution

This figure shows all the standard channels of distribution which a firm might use. Any route through the diagram is possible, including some which have not been drawn in. A firm tends to use channels which it thinks serve it well, but few firms of any size use only one route.

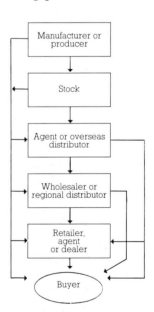

Source: *Business Studies: An Introduction* by David Dyer and Ian Chambers, Longman, 1987

● making comparisons

> – compare your findings with what the textbook says. Remember textbooks are not always right. (See Chapter 1, pages 1–2)

Reference books are useful for

- finding out background information on firms

  Example: To save asking lots of basic questions on a visit you could use a book such as *Key British Enterprises: The Top 20,000 British Companies*. You can find information on the type of trade; trading styles and names; markets; type of company; authorised and issued capital; number of employees and more!

- helping you to find information

  – some books are an index for lots of other reference sources.

  Example: *Business Statistics Index* (Pamela Foster, Headland Press, 1983) gives a guide to finding official and non-official statistics on a variety of topics – even frozen food!

- highlighting or emphasising a point

  Example: *Who's Who* lists the 'top' people in business, politics, entertainment and the military. To show that south-east England is relatively well off compared to other regions you could take a random sample of *Who's Who* entries and see where they live.

- improving the quality of your work

  – use a dictionary!

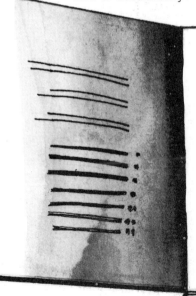

Reinforcing Research: Books

Rules   All data used must be

RELEVANT	— choose carefully
RELIABLE	— check up on accuracy
REVIEWED	— say why it's useful
REFERENCED	— use quotation marks and list all books used
RATIONED	— just use 'bits'

Organisations

...I'LL WRITE AND FIND OUT...

It's nice to see Dick back on the right track again!

You can seek information from organisations to help your investigations too. There are so many different organisations which might be helpful it is useful to divide them into five main groups.

- **private sector businesses** eg firms, including banks, building societies etc.
- **public sector businesses** eg British Coal, British Rail.
- **pressure groups** eg Trades Union Congress, Consumers Association, Shelter, Friends of the Earth.
- **government departments** eg Department of Trade and Industry, Department of the Environment.
- **government financed organisations** eg Equal Opportunities Commission, Citizens Advice Bureau.

There is a list of some other organisations on pages 111–115 but this is a very small proportion of the enormous number which exist. Most organisations produce publicity material and information, often free of charge. To collect material you can either visit the organisation or write to them enclosing a large stamped addressed envelope.

Here is an example of the kind of letter you might send –

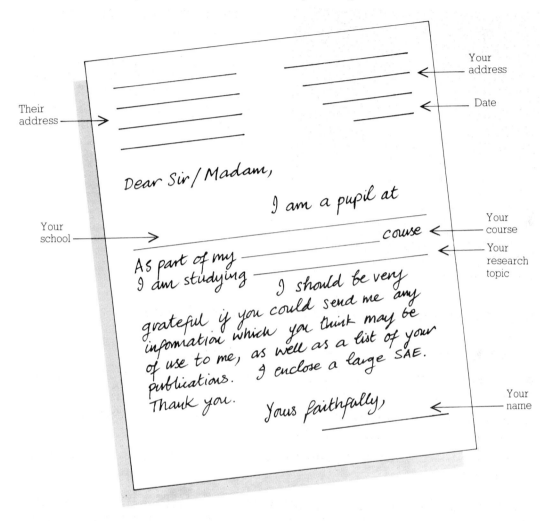

Their address →

Your school →

Your address ←
Date ←
Your course ←
Your research topic ←
Your name ←

Dear Sir / Madam,

I am a pupil at
_____
_____ course

As part of my _____
I am studying _____ I should be very
grateful if you could send me any
information which you think may be
of use to me, as well as a list of your
publications. I enclose a large SAE.
Thank you.

Yours faithfully,

| SPECIAL RESEARCH WARNING | △ | ORGANISATIONS |

1. Do you need to use all the information you've received?

Organisations will send you all kinds of information from advertising material to staff newspapers! This is more likely to happen when dealing with large organisations which have publicity or public relations departments. Don't feel you need to include all the material – only use it if your own work is improved by including the material.

2. Is the information reliable?

If it is publicity or advertising material then there must be some degree of bias towards the organisation. Material from organisations which are pressure groups, eg TUC, will also be biased. When you use information like this you must be critical about it and never include this type of material without your own comments.

3. Does the data improve your case?

Information from organisations can be used to

- collect specific information

    - this example is from a staff newspaper. It gives information about a new process and brings attention to it in a humorous way.

OK! We'll shrink wrap wallcovering, but we draw the *line* at Arthur's sandwiches.

The House of MayFair has taken a major step forward by combining their inspection and shrinkwrapping processes from separate operations into a single system. Basic operations now feed into two new Mark II Frastons and a M.A.F. shrinkwrapper. Before it was decided who would operate the new lines, all employee groups were consulted about job preferences. As a result it was agreed that the Frastons should be operated by the female labourforce of the shrink-wrapping bay.

Exercise 7

You are using the above extract in your coursework. Write a suitable comment to go with it.

- find information quickly and easily

    - banks, building societies and several other commercial organisations often produce reviews of interesting data and statistics. In the booklet shown on page 63 there are comparisons of prices, trade figures, consumer expenditure, etc.

- improve the presentation of your work

    Example: You could cut out pictures and information to make a
    point for you, or to brighten up your work. An example is
    shown at the top of page 64. Always add your own
    comment and don't include too much material.

BURBERRY TRADE MARK

Certain competitors of Burberrys Limited have recently made attempts to imitate BURBERRY merchandise. Copies have included the illegal use of our Designs and Registered Trade Marks. As a result of our objections, undertakings have been obtained from these firms that they will not repeat such infringements.

The words "BURBERRY" and "BURBERRYS" and the Mounted Knight device are the Registered Trade Marks of Burberrys Limited of London. Any unlawful action involving misuse of our Name, Designs or Registered Trade Marks or any other acts of unfair competition will result in legal action being taken to preserve our rights.

Burberrys
OF LONDON ®

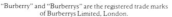

"Burberry" and "Burberrys" are the registered trade marks of Burberrys Limited, London.

Let it pour - shelter under the Burberry

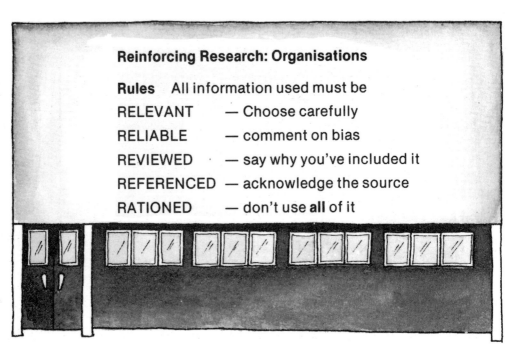

Reinforcing Research: Organisations

Rules   All information used must be

RELEVANT   — Choose carefully

RELIABLE   — comment on bias

REVIEWED   — say why you've included it

REFERENCED — acknowledge the source

RATIONED   — don't use **all** of it

6 Choosing research methods – following the leads

... I WONDER IF I CAN CHECK THESE ON THE POLICE COMPUTER...

You've come this far so you must agree that coursework is worthwhile. You've probably got an idea or even a hypothesis for your investigation. You know about the different methods of collecting data (evidence to us!). Now you need to decide which methods – it's likely that you'll need more than one – are best for 'following up the clues'.

Good investigators are **effective** – actually doing what they set out to do – and **efficient** – they don't waste time and effort doing it.

Dick Clever knows **broadly** what he wants to do – catch the thief – and to be effective and efficient he needs to break down his broad aim into a series of **specific** tasks such as – identify the owner of the fingerprints. When a specific or narrower task has been identified it becomes easier to choose the methods needed

- **observe** the fingerprint
- **interview** people at the scene of the crime
- **read** the police fingerprint files.

Dick Clever needed new information so he used observation and interviewing to collect primary data, and he was efficient in using police files to collect secondary data.

If you use the same process it will make it easier to choose the best method for your investigation. You know broadly what you want to do – test your hypothesis – and you can be effective and efficient by setting yourself a series of smaller tasks. Let's consider how the broad aim to test the hypothesis 'Foreign cars are more reliable than British cars' can be broken down. Some questions need to be asked.

- which cars should be compared?
- what does reliable mean?
- how can facts be collected on reliability?
- how can the results be presented?

The smaller tasks are based on these questions.

- **Choose which cars you want to compare**

    - OBSERVE the local traffic to choose a representative range of cars.

- **Decide what 'reliable' means**

    - INTERVIEW car owners, salespeople and garage mechanics for their opinion.
    - write to ORGANISATIONS such as the Automobile Association
    - read opinions and reports in MAGAZINES such as *Which?* and *What Car?*

- **Investigate the reliability of the cars you have chosen**

    - design a QUESTIONNAIRE to collect information on the reliability of the cars you want to compare.
    - use OFFICIAL STATISTICS to help you choose a representative sample of car owners, for example, *Social Trends* divides car owners into different income groups.

Who says foreign cars are more reliable than British cars?

- **Present your results in a way which is both interesting and convincing**

  - display your findings effectively by using tables, charts and graphs.
  - use quotations from INTERVIEWS and reports from NEWSPAPERS.
  - take **one** or **two** cuttings from MAGAZINES to brighten up any written work.

In this example primary and secondary data have been collected from a variety of sources and the main factor affecting the method chosen was the type of information needed.

Exercise 1

Consider the research project on health foods – Kate and Jane pages 12–13 and page 20. Break down their broad aim – to test their hypothesis 'Health foods cost more because the production is small scale' – into a series of smaller tasks.

You may have worked hard to break down your broad aim into a series of smaller tasks only to discover that a method you have chosen will neither be effective nor efficient. Consider the following factors – they may help you to avoid this situation.

- Has the information you want been collected already?

  If you want to be efficient don't waste time and effort seeking information which someone else has already collected. In other words, you can save on the 'legwork' by using a secondary source of data instead of a primary source, eg official statistics, textbooks or reference books, reports or handbooks produced by organisations.

- Do you need facts and figures?

  If you want information which can be shown in a graph or table you can use questionnaires, structured interviews or observation to collect primary data. This type of information is called **quantitative** data (ie data which can be quantified or put in the form of numbers).

- Are you interested in people's opinions?

  To collect primary data about what people think, for example, why they like a particular product, you would be better using an in-depth interview or participant observation rather than structured interviews or questionnaires. This type of data is called **qualitative** data (ie data with more depth and 'quality' than quantitative data).

- Have you got time to send out lots of questionnaires?

  If you have only a short time to complete your investigation using a questionnaire would not be a good idea. For instance, if the investigation is a homework assignment, by the time you design and test the questions the date for handing in the work will have arrived . . . and so will trouble if it's not ready! A quicker alternative would be to use structured interviews with some friends and relatives, or perhaps an observation.

- Are some methods of collecting information just impossible?

  There may be laws or regulations which mean certain methods cannot be used. You would not be allowed to observe in a nuclear reprocessing plant or down a mine because of safety regulations; some firms may refuse to give you information because it is confidential; copyright laws could stop you collecting some kinds of secondary data. Your teacher will give advice on these points.

- Will you be working by yourself?

  A greater amount of information can be collected if the investigation is a group project and this can influence the methods chosen. For example, a group could use structured interviews with a large sample, where an individual would need to send out questionnaires; an individual could choose participant observation as a main research method but a group could not.

● Is the research project big or small?

If your coursework involves several shorter assignments you may not have the opportunity to use a variety of methods which a longer project would allow. Longer projects let you use a mixture of qualitative and quantitative data from both primary and secondary sources.

Exercise 2

In each of the following situations suggest one method of collecting evidence which
    a) would be suitable; and
    b) should be avoided.

Give reasons for your suggestions.

1) How much influence has information technology had on retailing in the past 10 years?
2) Why do some food products have a bar code?
3) Who uses databases?

General investigations

Not all investigations are based on an hypothesis. There will be times when all you want to do is 'find out'. You might want to find out about a firm or topic just because you're interested, or you might want to see how something you learned about in class works in 'real life'; you could be 'fishing' for ideas for a research project, or you could quite simply be 'under teacher's orders'!

Whatever the reason for your investigation you'll need to write up what you find out. You can do this in two ways –

A **general report**, which will contain a variety of information gained from a wide area and this will show a breadth of knowledge and understanding. For example, if you have considered marketing as a general topic the results of your investigation may include information on types of markets, marketing methods, advertising, distribution etc. This type of research could be written up as a general report.

A **case study** is a particular case or example of a general topic. If the general topic was marketing then the case study would be a particular instance or example of marketing. For example, if you investigated the way by which a local clothing manufacturer markets its products, then this could be written up as a case study.

When writing a general report or a case study you must take special care to avoid simply describing, rather than analysing what you have found out. Give yourself the opportunity to consider the information you find and draw conclusions based on this information. This is called an **analysis of results** and is a VERY important part of coursework. (More about this in the next chapter.)

Choosing research methods

You should always be flexible about choosing research methods and this is particularly important in general investigations where you'll probably not have considered any methods beyond the first step. One method will often lead to another – in fact you'll be 'following the leads' for real!

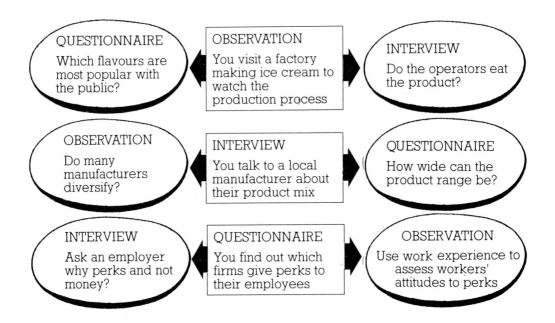

OBSERVATION
You visit a factory making ice cream to watch the production process

INTERVIEW
Do the operators eat the product?

OBSERVATION
Do many manufacturers diversify?

INTERVIEW
You talk to a local manufacturer about their product mix

QUESTIONNAIRE
How wide can the product range be?

INTERVIEW
Ask an employer why perks and not money?

QUESTIONNAIRE
You find out which firms give perks to their employees

OBSERVATION
Use work experience to assess workers' attitudes to perks

Coursework diary

Whichever research methods you use to follow leads it's always a good idea to keep a coursework diary. This is simply a brief record of activities and thoughts to do with your investigation. Use an exercise book so that you can make a note of any visits, the names of people you contacted, number of questionnaires sent out, books you have used and any thoughts, opinions or impressions you had. A diary is very useful if you are working in a group because it makes it easier to identify who did what. It could also come in useful if you lost any notes or evidence.

Feb 22
Visited planning officer
–not much good–couldn't
understand him. I'll
ask Dad's friend to
explain – I'm not scared
of him

Feb 27
See Dad's friend at
his office at 3.30pm.

7 Processing the evidence

During an investigation detectives build up their case by collecting and analysing evidence. The best detectives, such as you (and Dick!), **process** the evidence [PROCESS is detective for – describe – discuss – draw conclusions].

- DESCRIBE how the data was collected, comment on reliability.
- DISCUSS what the data shows – the main trends etc.
- DRAW CONCLUSIONS by **analysing your results** and relating them to the aims of your research.

All data should be well presented, but this is especially important when the coursework is part of an examination. By processing **all** data you will have clearly presented evidence of all research carried out. This is useful for identifying work done by different members of a group, and especially when the final presentation is in a non-written form.

Processing quantitative data

The clearest methods of presenting statistical data use tables, charts and graphs.

Tables

. . . show information in columns and rows and the reader can see quickly the type of data being presented and the trends shown in the data.

Example

RESEARCH TOPIC: the investigation of a possible market for a school coffee bar

Lunchtime arrangements of secondary school pupils

	BOYS		GIRLS		TOTAL
	Lower School	Upper School	Lower School	Upper School	
School lunch	29	14	15	4	62
Packed lunch	5	3	19	14	41
Fish & chip shop	3	11	2	0	16
Sandwich shop	4	18	7	23	52
Go home	9	4	7	9	29
	50	50	50	50	200

- The data were collected using questionnaires. The sample was made up of equal numbers of boys and girls, upper and lower school pupils. Each member of the group questioned 50 pupils. The registers were used as sampling frames. It was easy to collect lots of answers because we only wanted to ask people in school and there were four of us to do the work.

- The figures show what the pupils do for lunch. There are no alternatives other than those listed. The results show that about half the pupils go out of school at lunchtime and 70% of these pupils buy their lunch. Only 29% of upper school pupils take school lunch and 40% of all pupils staying at school bring a packed lunch.

- The sandwich shop seems to be the most popular 'out-of-school' choice, particularly among upper school pupils. The coffee bar plans to sell sandwiches and it looks like there could be a market for them. Almost half the pupils staying at school bring packed lunch, so they might like to have their lunch in a coffee bar instead of the dining hall. Lower school pupils tend to take school lunches, but they usually play table tennis etc at lunchtimes so they probably wouldn't use the coffee bar anyway.

Bar charts

. . . can be vertical or horizontal.

Example

RESEARCH TOPIC: an investigation of the range of retail services in the local area

Types of retail outlet in the town centre

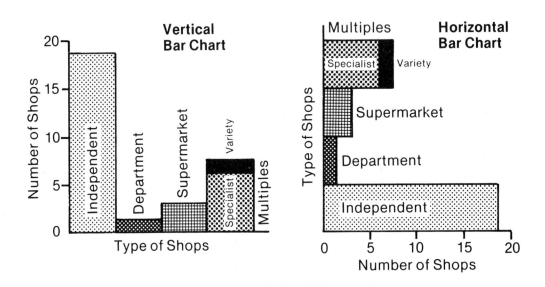

- This data was collected by observation. I just walked around the town centre counting the different types of shops. There were two shops I couldn't decide about so I asked the teacher when I got to school.

- Nearly all the shops are independent or multiples. The multiples are mostly specialist rather than selling a variety of goods. There is only one department store.

- The people are served mostly by independent shops so the choice of goods might be limited and the prices could be quite high. Big retailers might not be attracted to this town because it is small and near to a large city.

Pie charts

. . . are used to show proportions or percentages. For a pie chart you need to work out the angle for each 'slice', and work out the percentage so you can label the 'slice'. You'll need a calculator because 'real' research results are almost always awkward figures and you'll need to round them to the nearest whole number.

Example 1

RESEARCH TOPIC: investigating tastes in magazines

Results of survey – fashion 10   music 11
     adventure games 4   computers 2 $\left.\right\}$ 27 answers

Angles

fashion $\quad \dfrac{10}{27} \times 360° = 133°$

music $\quad \dfrac{11}{27} \times 360° = 147°$

adventure games $\dfrac{4}{27} \times 360° = 53°$

computers $\quad \dfrac{2}{27} \times 360° = \dfrac{27°}{360°}$

Percentages

$\dfrac{10}{27} \times 100 = 37\%$

$\dfrac{11}{27} \times 100 = 41\%$

$\dfrac{4}{27} \times 100 = 15\%$

$\dfrac{2}{27} \times 100 = \dfrac{7\%}{100\%}$

Tastes in magazines of pupils in 4R

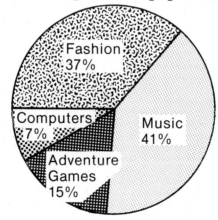

- I collected this data by asking the people in my class what kind of magazine they liked best.

- The chart shows that nearly half the sample bought music magazines. Not many people in the sample bought specialist magazines.

- Teenagers tend to buy fashion and music magazines more than any other kind.

Example 2 – where the results are already in percentages

RESEARCH TOPIC: survey of employment opportunities in the local area

Research results – primary 13%   secondary 30%   tertiary 57%

Angles

primary $\dfrac{13}{100} \times 360° = 47°$

secondary $\dfrac{30}{100} \times 360° = 108°$

tertiary $\dfrac{57}{100} \times 360° = \underline{205°}$
$\phantom{\dfrac{57}{100} \times 360° = }\underline{360°}$

Types of production in UK

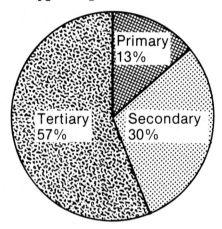

- I found this data in *An Economic Profile of Britain 1986*, published by Lloyds Bank, page 12. The teacher gave me the book.

- The figures show the share of total production carried out in three sectors of the UK economy. The figures are for 1984, but they probably haven't changed too much since then.

- National production tends to be mainly in the tertiary, or service, sector. Only 13% of production is primary. In the UK people must rely upon the tertiary sector for employment.

Line graphs

. . . are used to show information which has been collected over a period of time for different quantities. Time and quantities are always along the horizontal axis of the graph.

Example 1 – information collected over a period of time

RESEARCH TOPIC: types of finance available to firms

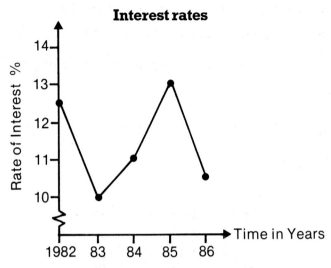

Interest rates

- I collected this data from the *Economic Progress Report*, Jan–Feb 1987, which I found in the school library.

- The graph shows the average interest rate for each year. I used a broken scale because the range wasn't very big. I don't think the figures are very accurate because I had to take them from a very small graph and I just guessed the average – the interest rate changed several times during a year – but they still show the general trend.

- The interest rate hasn't changed very much over the past five years. It has stayed quite high.

Example 2

RESEARCH TOPIC: enterprise project – making waffles

Costs and revenue of waffle production

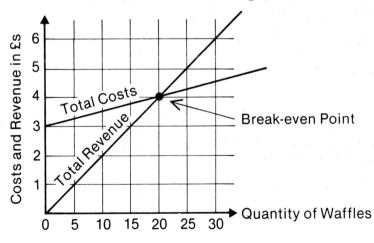

- The data was collected by calculating the costs of making the waffles – we got the prices from the local shops. We decided on a price of 20p per waffle because that was 5p cheaper than the prices in the shops, and then we worked out the possible revenue.

- The graph shows the total cost of making different quantities of waffles and the revenue that would be received from selling different quantities at 20p each.

- We would need to make and sell 20 waffles to break even. If we could sell more than 20 we would make a profit.

Exercise 1

Stephen was investigating the amount of space taken by advertising in different newspapers. He analysed 3 newspapers with the following results:

THIS IS NOT HOW TO MEASURE
COLUMN INCHES.

Courier (a 'free' newspaper) – 29% news and features;
Daily Mirror – 68% news and features;
Daily Telegraph – 82% news and features;

with the rest of the space being used for advertising.

Process this information using a table and a bar chart in your presentation.

Processing qualitative data

Qualitative data is not usually statistical but still needs to be clearly presented. You'll have collected this data during in-depth interviews and participant observation and not all of it will be relevant so just use what you need.

Headings

. . . that you used when you planned your interview or participant observation will be very useful. You can use quotations and examples under these headings as well as a description and analysis of what was said or observed.

Example

RESEARCH TOPIC: industrial relations in a local factory

Heading: Union Subscriptions

The employee pays £1.25 each week and this is taken off his wages before he gets them. He prefers paying this way because the subscription is paid regularly and he says it saves him the bother of having to remember to pay it.

- The data was collected during an in-depth interview with an employee who was very willing to answer my questions.
- It shows the way union subscriptions are collected and how much is paid.
- The advantage to the employee of this method of payment is not needing to remember the payment. It must be easier for the union representative too because he receives everybody's subscription at the same time without having to go and ask people.

Quotations

. . . can be used to highlight points and add colour, interest and reality to your research.

Example

RESEARCH TOPIC: types of business organisation

> 'I've got no time for worker co-operatives. They're OK so long as decisions don't have to be speedy, but when some customer wants an instant answer nobody will take the responsibility.'

- The quotation came from an in-depth interview with the winner of a local 'Businesswoman of the Year' competition. I interviewed her at her firm and there were lots of interruptions, such as the telephone ringing etc.

- She is giving her opinion on management in worker co-operatives. I meant to ask her if she traded with any but I forgot.

- It seems that people in worker co-operatives might lose business through not having bosses. This might only happen in large co-operatives and not be a problem in small ones. It might be that this woman has been let down by a co-operative and this has influenced her opinion.

Exercise 2

During an in-depth interview with the owner of a small factory Kevin wrote down this quotation:

'I could move the firm to the industrial estate and get the 10,000 square feet of factory space that I need, but if I do that I'll lose most of my work-force. I know that I could claim about £3000 for each person I recruit from the long-term unemployed register, but I depend heavily on skilled labour.'

Kevin's research topic is LOCATION OF FIRMS. Process this quotation for him.

Processing general descriptive information

This is the kind of information you collect which might describe processes or structures within a business, or give background information on the history of the firm or perhaps the range of product. You shouldn't spend a great deal of time on descriptive data – give a clear but brief presentation and concentrate on the analysis of your results.

Headings

. . . can be used to keep the presentation brief.

Example

RESEARCH AIM: marketing procedures in an international company

ORGANISATION: Private company
PARENT COMPANY: Forbo, Switzerland
AUTHORISED CAPITAL: £35,000
ISSUED CAPITAL: £31,000
NUMBER OF EMPLOYEES: 730

- This information was collected from the firm's brochures and by asking questions during an interview with a member of the marketing department.

- The information gives an idea of the size of the firm.

- I should be able to collect lots of data on marketing because it's a big firm and has overseas connections.

Diagrams

. . . can be used to show processes, organisational structures or layouts. Maps and photographs can also be used in this way.

Example

RESEARCH TOPIC: health and safety

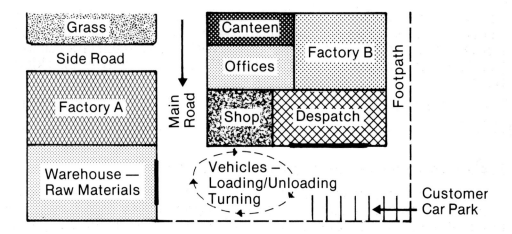

- The information was collected by observation at the firm.

- The diagram shows the general layout of the factory buildings and transport arrangements.

- The diagram will help to explain the reason for the firm's intention to move the factory shop to where the canteen is sited at present.

Processing secondary data

There are lots of different kinds of secondary data – as you saw in Chapter 5. Some of the ways by which this data is processed has already been discussed, such as the pie chart on page 75 and 76 and the line graph on page 77. You should take note that in both examples the description of how the data was collected also states **exactly** where the information came from. Secondary data must always be REFERENCED.

Quotations from secondary sources should be processed in the same way as quotations from in-depth interviews (see pages 79–80).

Cuttings

. . . from secondary sources can be used to give either specific or background information.

Example

RESEARCH TOPIC: product mix of a large firm

	AIRPORTS	BANKS	BARS/CLUBS	CANTEENS	CARAVANS	DEPARTMENT STORES/SHOPS	HEALTH CENTRES	HOMES	HOTELS	HOSPITALS	LABORATORIES	OFFICES	RESIDENTIAL HOMES	RESTAURANTS	SCHOOLS/UNIVERSITIES	SHIPS	SHOWROOMS	SPORTS COMPLEXES	SUPERMARKETS	TRAINS/BUSES
CUSHIONED VINYL/LINOLEUM FLOOR COVERINGS	•	•	•	•	•	•	•	•	•	•	•	•	•	•	•	•	•	•	•	•
WALLCOVERINGS	•	•	•	•	•	•	•	•	•	•	•	•	•	•	•		•			
SELF-ADHESIVE DECORATIVE VINYL				•	•			•								•	•			
UPHOLSTERY MATERIALS	•	•	•	•	•	•	•	•	•	•	•	•	•	•	•	•	•	•	•	•
CARPET TILES	•	•	•			•	•	•	•	•		•	•	•		•	•			
CURTAIN FABRICS	•	•	•	•	•	•	•	•	•	•	•	•	•	•	•	•	•	•	•	•
FACSIMILE REPRODUCTIONS	•	•	•	•		•	•	•	•	•	•	•	•	•	•	•	•	•	•	•

- This table was taken from an advertising leaflet which I collected from a firm.
- The table shows the range of products which one section of a firm makes. It shows where the products are used.
- This is a very neat way of showing the range of products and it will make it easier for me to explain points such as the firm's advertising methods. I can use this idea to show the product mix of all the firms I am comparing.

A final word on processing . . .

You found out in the last chapter how 'one method often leads to another'. Processing can help you to follow leads. Look back through this chapter and suggest follow-up action for some of the examples.

8 Presenting your case

The usual way of presenting coursework is in the form of a written project – but it doesn't have to be. Think of detective stories – you don't always have to read a book to find out 'who dunnit' . . . you can watch on television or at the cinema, read a comic or listen to a story on the radio. How are you going to present **your** case?

Presenting your case is all about communication – what is the most effective way for you to communicate? What is the best way for you to show the results of your hard work?

Now that you have thought about your own communication skills you need to look at the different ways of presenting your research project. Five possible methods of presentation are –

- WRITTEN PROJECT – this is the most often used method of presentation and if your coursework is for GCSE it may have to be in this form.

- DISPLAY – this could be a wall display or you could use a display board in the school library or reception area.

- ILLUSTRATED TALK – you could talk about your investigation and use diagrams, pictures and charts to emphasise points.

- DRAMA PRESENTATION – this would let you bring your research project to life by presenting situations 'as they really happened'.

- DEBATE – gives you the opportunity to clearly present the opposite points of view in an issue.

Exercise 2

In each of the following investigations suggest the different ways of presenting the case and the communication skills involved.

An investigation into an industrial dispute over the shortening of lunch breaks.

The effect of consumer protection laws on a manufacturer of gloves.

An investigation to decide whether it is better for firms to own their transport fleet or use a transport firm.

An investigation into the benefits a firm could gain by 'going public'.

Sometimes the method of presentation does not immediately fit the evidence and you may need to seek inspiration from your teacher or friends – but where there's a will . . . ! You could collect ideas by looking through books and magazines, visiting displays in your local library and shops, or by watching some television programmes. Sometimes you may have to change your original ideas about presentation if you want to show your results in the best possible way – so remember to **be flexible**.

Most coursework will be assessed and some will form part of GCSE assessment. It is important to keep a record of all your investigations and what you have found out – even if it was nothing! For example, if you visited a firm and you didn't find out any new information still make a note of this in your coursework diary. The most obvious reason for keeping accurate records is to help you with the final presentation but it is also important when you have worked in a group to be able to identify each group member's contribution.

YOU'LL BE FACED WITH A ~~MASS~~ MESS OF EVIDENCE

Let's suppose that your investigation is complete – what happens now? You'll be faced with a mass of evidence. There will be the primary data – the questionnaires (including the trial attempts); accounts of interviews; records of observations and results of any experiments. You'll have a variety of secondary data – leaflets, maps, newspaper cuttings and statistics. Also in your file will be your coursework diary and some 'extras'. The 'extras' could be the scrappy notes you made on visits; the script of the play you thought you might perform; a list of the books you have used; the title of a video you saw which you thought was relevant and almost everybody will have an interesting collection of bus tickets and sweet wrappers!

How are you going to use this evidence? Some guidelines for presenting all kinds of coursework are given in the **coursework summary** and this should help you to plan your presentation. Writing up a coursework summary is especially important if you are presenting your coursework in a non-written form as it will provide an account of what you have done and a statement of your reasons.

Coursework summary

Title

State the title of your coursework. This could be a single word, a question, a clever catchphrase or you might just want to state your hypothesis. It is sometimes easier to think of an exact title at the end of an investigation!

Introduction

I/we chose to investigate this area/topic because . . .
List all the reasons for your decision.

Hypothesis

First state your hypothesis – if you have one. If you don't then state the general aim of your investigation.

I/we decided upon this hypothesis (or general aim) because . . .
Keep your reasons brief, you've already given your reasons for choosing this particular investigation.

Research methods

The research methods used for this coursework are . . .
List the methods with a brief description – a single sentence about each will be enough.

I/we used these methods because . . .

Personal research experiences

The research was easy/difficult/boring/fun etc because . . .
Say what you feel – if you thought it was a waste of time then say so, but you must also say **why** it was a waste of time.

I/we think that research of this topic could be improved by . . .
– and everybody can complete this sentence because there's always room for improvement!

Method of presentation

I/we decided to present the results of the research in the form of . . .
because . . .
Give all your reasons for choosing a particular method of presentation – show why it was best for you – explaining how the advantages outweighed the disadvantages.

Conclusions

I/we think that the hypothesis is true/not true because . . .
Don't go into too much detail here, testing the hypothesis was the purpose of the research.

If you have a general aim, briefly sum up the main conclusions you have drawn from your investigation and suggest reasons for some of your results.

Possible further research

Research into some topics can be extended in other directions – consider your topic in this way.

If I/we were to continue to investigate this topic I/we could . . .
Ask these questions/look at this area/become a leading expert/enjoy discovering/become bored? Whatever the answer – remember you must explain your reasons.

When the coursework summary has been completed you'll have an overall picture of your coursework. Now you can start to sort through the evidence and decide what is relevant and what is not. Don't throw anything away yet – except perhaps the bus tickets and sweet wrappers!

Written projects

Usually the term 'coursework' brings to mind the idea of a written project. Some students may prefer to present their coursework as a written project and some examination boards may insist that coursework for GCSE examinations is to be in the written form. How should you start writing a project? Here's some hints –

1. Decide which is the best order to present your research findings. Think about a series of headings and use these to divide your work – perhaps you could use the specific tasks which break down your hypothesis (see Chapter 6). Make sure that the order is sensible – don't put the conclusion before the results!
2. Make sure that the important parts of each section stand out. You don't need to have 'pop-up' charts or centrefolds but photographs and coloured illustrations will help to emphasise certain aspects. Similarly newspaper and magazine cuttings can be used to illustrate – but don't overdo it and don't use cuttings instead of evidence. Keep any spare cuttings in a folder – you, or someone in your class, may find them useful later.
3. Write one section at a time and in rough first. Give yourself plenty of time to go back and read your work through again – you may have

written on a day when your creative writing skills were not quite at their best!

4. When you're more or less happy with the first draft ask a friend or a teacher to read through and invite them to make **constructive criticisms**. Constructive criticism means the criticism is balanced by a suggestion of how to improve the coursework. Remember this when you are asked to read through other people's work – be constructive – anyone can be negative and that doesn't help the writer at all.

5. The final version – don't get over-excited just because you've finished – remember the basics. You need to include a table of contents (at the front!), and an Appendix (at the back!) which contains all the evidence that doesn't fit neatly into the actual project. Have a nice design on the front cover and be careful about your spelling – 'BUISNESS STUDYS' does not look very impressive! Take care when numbering the pages – all the numbers should be at the top or at the bottom but not a mixture of both. Use the punch for making holes carefully – don't have photographs, paper etc escaping. Take care to keep your work clean – the topic may have been a fish and chip business but your project doesn't have to smell like one. Finally, be proud of what you have done – it will represent a lot of hard work and effort.

You may decide that you do not want to present your case in the form of a written project but prefer to give a talk or put on a display. If you do make this decision then you must be very careful to keep a detailed file of evidence and an up-to-date coursework diary. Your coursework summary should be thoroughly prepared and well-presented. This will help your teacher to assess your coursework and will also provide a record of your efforts for the examination board.

Display

A library or wall display lets the pictures tell the story. Your research findings are presented visually with as few words as possible so it is important to use well-designed charts and snappy slogans. So if you are the kind of person for whom a picture paints a thousand words, read on –

1. When using display keep the subject or topic quite narrow. If you don't you may need to use so much display space that your coursework becomes adopted as a route for a fun run!
2. Use the coursework summary to help you to identify the main points of your investigation.
3. If the display shows a sequence of events make sure that you identify the beginning and the end.
4. The display material should be high quality. If you intend using

newspaper or magazine cuttings stick them on card and cover with plastic film. Attach explanatory notes to **all** diagrams and pictures and check the spellings on labels and titles. You can't make your display vandal-proof but you can take out some insurance by keeping duplicates of material used and taking photographs of the display as soon as it is completed.

5. Your school will only have a limited amount of space for display so make sure that it will be convenient to present your coursework in this way.

Illustrated talk

You'll be standing up in front of your class and telling them about your investigation. You can use photographic slides, blackboard diagrams, overhead projector transparancies or models to illustrate your talk. It's also a good idea to have a 'Question Time' at the end of your talk. If the talk needs to be assessed, arrange for an audio- or video tape to be taken.

1. The coursework summary will help you to plan the order of topics. List the main headings.
2. Make brief notes to guide you through the talk. Small cards with headings can be turned over quite easily. Remember to make a note of when to introduce photographs, diagrams etc.
3. Do not include irrelevant material – it will distract your audience.
4. Prepare illustrations carefully. Make sure that any equipment is in good working order – check the projector bulb and the batteries for the cassette.
5. Stay to the point – don't ramble. Sound cheerful – not bored. Keep it short.
6. To make sure the Question Time is successful, be cunning and arrange with a couple of friends to ask questions which will get things going.
7. Before you give your talk, take a deep breath and be determined to enjoy what you are doing. Speak slowly and clearly and you'll be so good that they might even ask for your autograph!

Drama presentation

At some time during your life you will have been involved in a role play. Role play means pretending to be someone else and behaving how you think they would behave in a certain situation, for example you may pretend to be a bank manager interviewing a client who has asked for a loan. During the play you will identify the personal qualities the bank manager will be looking for in the client. You will also be able to give the audience some factual information about bank loans such as what is meant by the rate of interest and which assets can be used as collateral. A play would be a good way to show what you have discovered about the communication channels in a firm or the activities of consumer pressure groups. To use this method of presentation you must plan carefully and show a willingness to work as a team.

1. Set up a good working arrangement – either choose a leader or agree to be responsible for different tasks. If the coursework is to be assessed your teacher must know exactly what each group member is doing.
2. Use the coursework summary to identify events or situations which will present your aims and conclusions most effectively.

3. Before starting to write the script or order of events it might help to watch a video or television programme where the results of an investigation have been dramatised. For example, the Barclays Bank video in which John Cleese opens a bank account – note how the main points are emphasised.
4. Agree with the group on the final script and stick to the joint decision – this is a **team** effort.
5. Make sure that you have all the props and that you're well-rehearsed – you have to be professional or the audience could become bored – and possibly rowdy!

Debate

This is a good way to present two sides of an issue. If you are good at arguing then you should do well, but remember you'll need to find an opposition who will co-operate.

1. The two sides or 'houses' must agree on a single aim or hypothesis. One side will set out to prove the hypothesis while the other will try to disprove it.
2. The research findings may or may not support your argument so you will need to be quite selective with the material you use. The coursework summary can help you with this.
3. Keep your evidence neat and tidy because you may need to make quick reference during the debate and if you are asked questions from the 'floor'.
4. Ask an independent person to control the debate.
5. Concentrate on convincing your audience that your case is the best through the evidence you present rather than by using gimmicks.

The methods of presentation discussed should show you that your coursework need not always be written, and that the presentation can be fun! Often in the business world written communications are used only as a 'back-up' or confirmation of oral communications – you could use your coursework summary like this – the confirmation of what you found out in your research.

9 Detectives' disasters

'Dear Dick...HELP...signed Desperate'

Sometimes no matter how careful you are in your planning and preparation something goes wrong. Sorry we can't offer a 'help-line', but it might help if you know that you're not the only one it happens to . . .

Dear Dick

I spent ages working on the design of my questionnaire and working out who should fill one in before I delivered them. That was 3 weeks ago and I haven't even got half of them back. My work has to be handed in next week!

(Lost, Luton)

Dear Lost

I assume you made careful arrangements for collecting the questionnaires – these things happen. Analyse the ones you've got and include a statement about why your results might not be accurate. In your conclusions mention this problem pointing out that this is one of the disadvantages of using questionnaires and describe how you would change your method if you did this research again.

Dear Dick

I wanted to find out something new and exciting but the results of my investigation have ended up being totally predictable – as always.

(Explorer, Epsom)

Dear Explorer

You must not be disheartened. At this stage you should be concentrating on developing your research skills rather than discovering new information. Don't expect too much from your research at present – you should be pleased that you're getting the same results as the experts!

Dear Dick

I thought I was going to have plenty of time to write up my results but I caught measles and I haven't got enough time now.

(Spotty, Swansea)

Dear Spotty

You'll have to discuss this with your teacher – you may get an extension because of your illness. But don't leave it until the last minute next time, write up results as soon as possible.

Dear Dick

I was getting along really well with my research. It was really interesting and I'd collected stacks of notes, including questionnaires. Then while I was away for the weekend my Mum cleaned my bedroom and threw the notes and my coursework diary out. What can I do?

(Depressed, Derby)

Dear Depressed

I know how you feel – I used to have a cleaner just like your Mum. Take a blank sheet of paper and write your hypothesis at the top in big letters. Make a note of everything you can remember finding out and list it under two headings – 'PROVES' and 'DISPROVES'. Go through the lists, cross off what cannot be collected again. Collect what evidence you can and write a description of the evidence that's lost. Show this to your teacher – it might be OK – at least there won't be any irrelevant data!

Dear Dick

Most of the information I've collected is irrelevant. Help!

(Worried, Wolverhampton)

Dear Worried

Well done for spotting this! You can write up your results as a general report or you could think up a new hypothesis.

Dear Dick

I'm half-way through my project and the firm I was investigating has gone out of business – I've got nothing left to investigate.

(Abandoned, Aberdeen)

Dear Abandoned

Don't give up – you have lots to investigate! Your teacher will help you to work out a new hypothesis and you can investigate why the firm went bankrupt. Remember, always be flexible.

Dear Dick

I'm really interested in computers and I thought doing research on 'computers in manufacturing' would be good – but it's really boring and I can't make any progress. How can I get this project finished quickly?

(Bored, Bournemouth)

Dear Bored

You need to find some fun to put into your work. Why not store your results on disc? If you like messing around with computers you could use your expertise to display your results in an original and clever way. You'll have so much fun that you'll be rushing to collect information so that you can write it up!

Dear Dick

I'm sick of coursework. Every subject I do has coursework and I'm sick of it. I never seem to have any time to myself and we always have work for the holidays.

(Overworked, Oxford)

Dear Overworked

Think of it as character-building!

10 Unsolved cases

Learner detectives often need some help to get started with investigations. The following examples have been tried before (with a wide variety of outcomes!) and should give you some ideas you can follow, adapt or use just as a framework.

Example 1: Job satisfaction

Aim

To investigate job satisfaction.

Hypothesis

People just work for the money.

Method

You need to find out about workers' job attitudes.

Two steps are involved in this survey

- designing a questionnaire, and
- choosing a suitable sample.

Make a list of the reasons why you think people work and construct closed questions to count up the answers. You will also need some open questions to collect detailed opinions and any additional information. Here is an example of this type of questionnaire (part only):

In each of the following questions tick the box which is closest to your view:

Question 1

A good job depends on	Strongly Agree	Agree	Don't know	Disagree	Strongly Disagree
1 Promotion prospects					
2 Interesting work					
3 Friendly workmates					
4 Lots of perks					
5 Above average wages					

Question 2

Which of the above factors is the <u>most</u> important (give number) _____

Question 3

Which factor(s) do you think are missing from the list above?

_____

_____

A representative sample of people will include workers from each main group of the working population. To help you choose the groups you will need to research the different ways in which workers are classified. You can do this by using a textbook or official statistics from publications such as *Social Trends* or the *Employment Gazette*. An example of groups could be – 'management & middle management'; 'skilled & semi-skilled'; 'unskilled'. Remember to include both men and women in your sample.

Presentation and analysis of results

Sort your evidence by collecting the results of your questionnaire. You could present Q1 in the form of a table.

Factors	% of sample whose views were closest to:				
	Strongly Agree	Agree	Don't know	Disagree	Strongly Disagree
1	20%	35%	35%	5%	5%
2	50%	20%	10%	20%	—
3					
4					
5					

Make a general statement about the most important factors.

You can use Q2 to point out the single most important factor. It may be that when people are forced to choose one factor your results from Q1 are changed.

The answers to Q3 can be used to criticise your research method and suggest future improvements.

Part of your analysis could include a comparison of attitudes between different groups with you commenting on possible reasons for the differences.

Most important factors

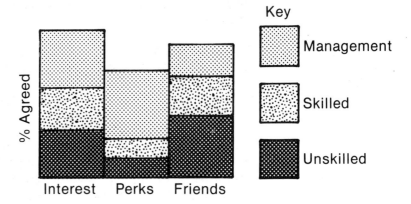

98

Possible further research	Use different sample groups to compare, such as industrial and service workers; compare men with women; compare part time workers with full time.
	Arrange in-depth interviews with people who have made unusual changes in career or people who change jobs quite often.

Example 2: Trends in retailing

Aim	To investigate the changing trends in retailing.
Hypothesis	People prefer to shop in hypermarkets.
Method	Use a questionnaire to investigate people's shopping preferences. You will need to find out where they shop regularly, their opinions of hypermarkets regarding prices, variety of goods, opening hours, other services such as cashpoints and cafes, car parking facilities. Other information which might prove useful would be how far shoppers travel to shop at a hypermarket, the method of transport used and where they buy 'everyday' goods such as bread, milk, fruit and vegetables.
	You could give the questionnaire to friends and relatives, or you could ask a sample of shoppers from a hypermarket. If you want to ask shoppers you will need to ask permission from the store managers and then make arrangements to do the survey. If you are going to ask the public remember to keep your questionnaire short and try to use closed questions where possible.
Presentation and analysis of results	You could show the percentage of people who prefer to shop at hypermarkets as a fraction such as – 'only 1 in every 6 shoppers prefer to . . .' or '9 out of 10 shoppers . . .' – depending upon your results.
	The most popular features of hypermarkets could be displayed in the form of a bar chart and you could emphasise certain findings using pie charts. For example, you might want to draw attention to the method of transport people use to travel to hypermarkets, or the type of goods bought –

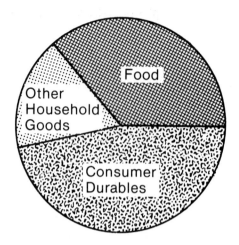

From your research can you suggest what the future trends might be? Do you think hypermarkets will become more or less popular? Has your research shown any services which hypermarkets could improve upon?

Possible further research

Find out why some hypermarkets are more popular than others.

Compare other types of retailing.

How might a change in the laws regarding Sunday trading affect hypermarkets?

Example 3: Health and safety regulations

Aim

To investigate how health and safety regulations are applied in a firm.

Hypothesis

Health and safety regulations cannot prevent all industrial accidents.

Method

You first need to find out about the 'Health and Safety at Work Act, 1974'. This is a complicated document so it would be a good idea to first look at a textbook and find out the main areas covered by the Act. Many firms produce leaflets and handbooks to tell employees about the regulations and collecting some of these would be helpful. Every school or college has a member of staff who has responsibility for health and safety – you could arrange an in-depth interview with this person to help you to collect information.

Once you have a basic knowledge of what you are looking for you could arrange to visit a firm and observe the health and safety precautions which are applied. While visiting the firm you could interview the Safety Officer to find out if there are any particular hazards which need special attention, such as guards on machines or employees needing to wear protective clothing.

It may be difficult to get details about any industrial accidents from the firm, especially if this information is confidential. You can overcome this problem to a certain extent by asking friends and relatives if they have any experience of industrial accidents; by looking for examples in the newspapers; and using your observation to spot potential hazards.

Presentation and analysis of results

Results could be presented in the form of a booklet and/or wall display which encourages people to become safety conscious. You could include some examples of industrial accidents to 'frighten' people! You'll probably have interviewed lots of people during your research so don't forget to make good use of quotations.

If your research project is to be assessed for GCSE you will need to prepare a statement on whether or not your hypothesis was proved, and include details of the evidence which supports your opinion. (See page 89).

Possible further research

You could investigate other laws associated with the protection of employees, such as The Offices, Shops and Railway Premises Act, 1963.

You could find out about the costs to employers involved in obeying the laws, and the costs involved in ignoring them.

Example 4: Database of local firms

Aim

To create a database of local firms.

Hypothesis

None.

Method

This general investigation of local firms could be carried out by a group in which each student has responsibility for a particular area or type of firm.

You will need to decide upon the size of the area. Using a large scale Ordnance Survey map an area could be marked out, for example 1, 2, 3, or whatever -mile radius of the school. If the area does not have many firms you could use the local authority boundary to mark out a much larger area.

A list of firms in the area should be compiled. This can be done by using local directories which may be available from the local council. If you want to collect a substantial amount of information you could send questionnaires to the firms, or interview by visiting or telephoning firms. For larger firms you could save the 'legwork' by using reference books such as *The Top 20,000 British Companies.*

The firms could be classified according to

- sector – primary, secondary, tertiary.
- type of production – extractive, manufacturing etc
- organisation – private or public limited company, partnership etc.
- number of employees – 1–50, 51–100, 101–150 etc.
- any other classification you think might be useful.

Presentation and analysis of results	The information could be stored in electronic data-files. You could use a commercial program such as DATABASE (Acornsoft) or VIEWSTORE, or you might be able to create your own. From this database specific information could be selected and displayed in the form of bar charts, pie charts, tables or colour coding on a map.
Possible further research	The regular updating of information would be necessary.
	Introduce different classifications.
	Increase the geographical area.
	Investigate the possibility of marketing the database you have created.

Example 5: Advertising expenditure

Aim	To investigate patterns of advertising expenditure.
Hypothesis	Sweets are advertised more than any other product.
Method	Collecting information for a project like this can take a long time and it might be a good idea to work in a group. You need to examine the main methods of advertising and find out how often products are advertised.

- Watch both ITV and Channel 4 and note the products which are advertised and the time. You could divide this task by giving group members different times to watch. The observation is best if it can be done every day for a week.

- Choose a sample of magazines to analyse. Use the more general type of magazine such as those aimed at women, teenagers and children. If you choose specialist magazines your results will be affected, for example sweets will not be advertised in slimming magazines! You could analyse the amount of advertising space used for each type of product.

- Choose a sample of national newspapers and analyse the space used for advertising in the same way as suggested for magazines.

- Survey the posters in your area noting the number of times products are advertised. Write to the Advertising Association for information on advertising expenditure.

Presentation and analysis of results

You could present the results in the form of tables.

Television					
Time	Number of times advertised				
	Sweets	Convenience snacks/food	Clothes	Cars	Pet food
7– 9 am 9–11 am 11– 1 pm 1– 3 pm etc					

Magazines, newspapers and posters					
Title	% share of total advertising space				
	Sweets	Convenience snacks/food	Clothes	Cars	Pet food

Do the figures support your hypothesis? Are there any results which surprise you? Can you suggest reasons for your results? How do your results compare with the information from the Advertising Association?

Possible further research

Investigate the amount of advertising done by the different producers of similar products.

Examine the techniques used by advertisers by analysing the products associated with hero worship, sex appeal etc.

Example 6: Raising finance

Aim

To investigate methods by which small firms can raise finance and prepare a case study.

Hypothesis

None.

Method

You will need to find out the different methods of raising finance that are generally available. Use a textbook to make a list of broad headings. Once you have an idea of the range of possible sources you can arrange an interview with, or write to the Economic Development Officer at your local authority. (This person might have a different title in your authority so check first with your teacher.) You could also write to the Small Firms Information Centre which is run by the Department of Trade and Industry – the address of your local office will be in the telephone directory. Information leaflets are also available from CRAC/Hobsons Press Ltd – *Starting a New Business* and Barclays Bank plc – *Working for Yourself*, addresses on pages 112 and 113.

When you've collected this data you'll find that not all sources of finance are available to small firms. It would be a good idea to interview some people who have recently started their own businesses and ask them how easy it was to raise finance.

Note If you state clearly when requesting the interview that you're only interested in methods of raising finance and **not** confidential matters, such as amounts, there's a better chance of you being given an interview.

Not a recommended method of raising finance!

Presentation and analysis of results

You could prepare a fact sheet on methods of finance available. Point out that a small firm can use only some of these and list them separately. Take each method in turn discussing whether in 'real life' small firms can raise finance using these methods. Use your interview results to help add reality to the case study.

Make sure that you use headings to organise the case study and acknowledge quotations.

Possible further research

Interview the owner of a small business which has been running for some years and compare the methods of raising finance when the business started, to methods today.

Interview a bank manager to find out what factors they take into account when someone asks for finance either to start or expand a small firm. Prepare a 'guide to borrowing' for young entrepreneurs.

Example 7: Using an enterprise project as coursework for assessment

> At Tynedale high school 15 enterprising youngsters raised £71 for Esther Rantzen's Childline Appeal through a Christmas Kissogram service at 30p a time.
>
> Source: *The Times Educational Supplement* 28.3.87

Lots of schools are involved in enterprise projects. Some projects are long running, eg tuck shops, while others are short projects, eg mince pies at Christmas. These projects can be broken down into separate assignments so that the group members can identify their contribution and then the coursework can be assessed. Keeping coursework diaries up to date is absolutely essential. The following example is a suggestion of how an enterprise project can be used for assessment.

General aim

To organise and carry out an enterprise project which provides a Kissogram service.

Project 1

Aim

To investigate the cost of providing the service and estimate its profitability.

106

Method	Make a list of the materials needed to provide the service. This will include costumes, stationery, advertising materials, possible transport eg collecting costumes or information, rent for 'stalls' in the school's main hall and corridors. Collect information about the cost of these items by surveying prices in the shops and mail order; collect prices for hiring and making costumes. The rent will have to be 'negotiated' with your headteacher!
Presentation and analysis of results	Estimate the total costs and show on a graph. Decide on two possible prices and calculate the revenue which would be raised by selling different quantities of Kissograms. Show the estimated total revenue on the graph. Identify the break-even point for each price. Draw conclusions from your research about whether the service can be provided and make a profit. Write a report to the rest of the group explaining the basis of your calculations.

Project 2

Aim	To investigate the market for a Christmas Kissogram service.
Method	Prepare a questionnaire to find out how many pupils and staff would use the service. Find out what 'variety' of Kissogram would be the most popular, and how much buyers would be prepared to pay. Choose a suitable sample and then conduct the survey.
Presentation and analysis of results	Analyse the questionnaires to find out if the service would be used, which varieties would be the most popular and the probable price. Present your results in a suitable form eg bar chart. Use the break-even points from Project 1 to estimate the profit/loss the service would make. Write a report to the rest of the group and in it outline your survey methods and results, your recommendations and the calculations on which you have based your decision.

Project 3

Aim	To advertise the Christmas Kissogram service

Method	Investigate the advertising techniques used by commercial Kissogram firms to help you to plan the campaign. Plan an advertising campaign using posters and leaflets. Work out the cost of the advertising and check that it is within the original budget. Before advertising consider the consumer protection laws related to advertising, and the advice given by the Advertising Standards Authority and make sure that your advertising campaign is within the guidelines.
Presentation and analysis of results	The final presentation will be the posters and the leaflets used in the advertising campaign but for assessment you will need to be able to provide 'proof' of research. Your coursework diary will provide a record and you should have processed every piece of evidence gathered. You should have the results of your investigation of commercial firms; the information you collected when you worked out the cost of advertising; the results of your investigation of consumer protection and an actual leaflet produced. You could photograph the posters. Make sure that each piece of evidence is well presented, eg show the costs in the form of a table and use headings to write up the results of the consumer protection research.

Project 4

Aim	To recruit 'staff' for the Kissogram service.
Method	Investigate the methods used by commercial firms to recruit staff. Prepare a job description to give to people who are interested. Advertise for staff. Consider the applications carefully and interview the people you think might be most suitable. You must prepare a contract of employment in case the staff change their mind at the last minute!
Presentation and analysis of results	This project is similar to Project 3 in that the final presentation is non-written. You will need to keep an accurate record of research in your coursework diary and make sure that each investigation is clearly written up. You should have the results of your investigation into methods of advertising for staff – don't forget to include your own comments. Keep a copy of the job description and employment contract and any information you had to gather to learn how to produce

them. You could tape the interviews and give a written comment on these.

Note If there is more than one person speaking on the tape make sure that you identify yourself before you start to speak.

Project 5

Aim Selling Kissograms.

Method You will need to design booking forms and receipts. It's probably a good idea to investigate how commercial firms handle bookings eg home services, such as carpet and upholstery cleaning, repair services etc. You could interview people who work in these types of firm to try and find out how problems like overbooking and running behind schedule can be avoided. You will need to conduct a survey to see which would be the 'best' site for the stalls. This could be done by observing the movement in the school at breaks, lunchtime, before and after school. Sell the Kissograms and make suitable arrangements to bank the money.

Presentation and analysis of results

Include a booking form in your presentation and explain how the design was decided upon – you will need to include the results of any interviews and investigations. You should also include a discussion of problems you could have met and how you avoided them and also discuss problems which you did have. Present the results of the investigation into the siting of the stalls using charts and diagrams. Show the results of trading Kissograms in the form of a profit and loss account, or as a balance sheet with explanatory notes.

Appendix: List of useful addresses

This list represents only a small number of the organisations which might provide information relevant to your research. You may get other ideas for addresses from your teacher or local reference library. (An example of the kind of letter you could write is given on page 61).

When you write for information remember the following points:

- Find out if the organisation can help you **before** you write.
- Make sure you say **exactly** what kind of information you want – if it's general information, then say so.
- Enclose a large stamped addressed envelope unless otherwise stated.
- If the organisation has a local branch, write to them – it might be quicker and more successful.
- Address your letters to the Information Department of the organisation unless otherwise stated.
- Don't be disheartened if you don't receive replies.

General

- Your local council can provide a wide range of information – it's always worth checking with your teacher which department you should write to, eg if you want information about refuse collection you should write to the Environmental Department.

- The Trades Union Congress will give you information on all aspects of employment and industrial relations including race, gender, unemployment and new technology.

    Trades Union Congress
    Congress House
    Great Russell Street
    London WC1B 3LS

- The Office of Population Censuses and Surveys produces official statistics and other information on issues which are of concern to the government.

    OPCS Information Branch
    St Catherines House
    10 Kingsway
    London WC2B 6JP

- The Department of Trade and Industry collects statistics on several aspects of business including consumer credit, imports etc.

  Department of Trade and Industry
  Business Statistics Office Library
  Room 1.001
  Government Buildings
  Cardiff Road
  Newport
  Gwent NP9 1XG

but if you want general information write to your local office or

  The Headquarters Library of the Department of Trade and Industry
  LG 16
  1 Victoria Street
  London SW1H 0ET

Consumer affairs

Citizens Advice Bureau

– look in your local telephone directory.

Office of Fair Trading
Field House (Room 310c)
15–25 Bream's Buildings
London EC4A 1PR

Consumers' Association
14 Buckingham Street
London
WC2N 6DS

Enterprise

Young Enterprise
Robert Hyde House
48 Bryanston Square
London W1A 1BQ

CRAC Learning Materials
Hobsons Publishing plc
Bateman Street
Cambridge
CB2 1LZ

Enterprise Education Unit
Durham University Business School
Mill Hill Lane
Durham DH1 3LB

Financial

Barclays Bank plc
Public Relations Department
54 Lombard Street
London EC3P 3AH

The Bank of England Information
   Division
Threadneedle Street
London
EC2R 8AH

The Building Societies Association
3 Savile Row
London W1X 1AF

Inland Revenue Education Service
PO Box 10
Wetherby
West Yorks LS23 7EH

The Stock Exchange
Old Broad Street
London EC2N 1HP

Banking Information Service
10 Lombard Street
London EC3V 9AT

Industry

Mrs Jan Hussey
Information Officer
Understanding British Industry
Sun Alliance House
New Inn Hall Street
Oxford
OX1 2QE

Unilever Educational Liaison
PO Box 68
Unilever House
London EC4 4BQ

BP Educational Service
PO Box 5
Wetherby
West Yorkshire LS23 7EH

(Free information can be provided
only for the following topics:-
oil–exploration, production, refin-
ing, petrochemicals; coal–gas;
solar power. A catalogue listing
other materials at subsidised
prices is available.)

International relations

United Nations Information Centre
20 Buckingham Gate
London SW1E 6LB

European Parliament
Information Office
2 Queen Anne's Gate
London SW1H 9AA

Campaign for Nuclear
  Disarmament
22–24 Underwood Street
London N1 7JG

Council for Education in World
  Citizenship
Seymour Mews House
Seymour Mews
London W1H 9PE

Mass media

Advertising Association
Abford House
15 Wilton Road
London SW1V 1NJ

Advertising Standards Authority
Brook House
2–16 Torrington Place
London WC1E 7HN

Information Office
Independent Broadcasting
  Authority
70 Brompton Road
London SW3 1EY

Programme Correspondence
  Section
British Broadcasting Corporation
Broadcasting House
Portland Place
London W1A 1AA

Campaign for Press and
  Broadcasting Freedom
9 Poland Street
London W1V 3DG

Politics

Conservative Party
32 Smith Square
London SW1P 3HH

Labour Party
150 Walworth Road
London SE17 1JT

Liberal Party
1 Whitehall Place
London SW1A 2HE
(send large SAE)

Social Democratic Party
4 Cowley Street
London SW1P 3NB

Local Government Information Unit
1/5 Bath Street
London EC1V 9QQ

Work and unemployment

Confederation of British Industry
Centre Point
103 New Oxford Street
London WC1A 1DU

Manpower Services Commission
Moorfoot
Sheffield S1 4PQ

Unemployment Unit
9 Poland Street
London W1V 3DG
(send large SAE)

TUC see General

Miscellaneous

Equal Opportunities Commission
Overseas House
Quay Street
Manchester M3 3HN

Commission for Racial Equality
Elliot House
10/12 Allington Street
London SW15 1EH

National Association of Youth
    Clubs
Keswick House
30 Peacock Lane
Leics LE1 5NY

Low Pay Unit
9 Upper Berkeley Street
London W1H 8BY

Friends of the Earth
377 City Road
London EC1V 1NA

Shelter
157 Waterloo Road
London SE1 8XF